ICONS

GORDANA BABIC

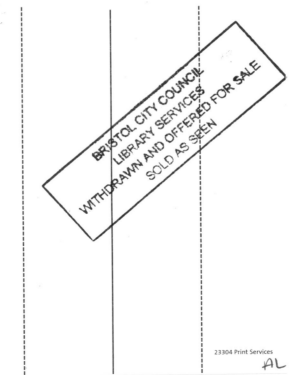
STUDIO EDITIONS
LONDON

PUBLISHED BY STUDIO EDITIONS
PRINCESS HOUSE, 50 EASTCASTLE STREET
LONDON W1N 7AP
ENGLAND

COPYRIGHT © 1988 BY PROEX PROSVETA, BELGRADE
PRODUCTION PROEX PROSVETA

EDITORS: IVAN NINIĆ
NATAŠA TANASIJEVIĆ-POPOVIĆ

ENGLISH TRANSLATION
MADGE TOMAŠEVIĆ

ISBN 1 85170 216 4

PRINTED AND BOUND IN YUGOSLAVIA

For centuries the icon has had its place in European culture, both as a religious object and as a work of art. In some periods highly prized and venerated, in others disputed and destroyed, it has played a prominent role in the Christian period in the East and in western Europe. People have laid down their lives both in the defence of icons and in their destruction. In the Byzantine Empire, in the age of iconoclasm (726–843), greater importance was attached to them than to human life. However, in the first centuries A.D., when the new faith appeared and spread throughout the Roman Empire, Christians rejected paintings, sculpture and any other symbolic representation of their religious beliefs, displaying a repugnance towards the ancient pagan custom of worshipping idols. There is not a single painting, relief or monument than can be identified as a work of Christian art predating A.D. 200.

Spreading clandestinely in the age of imperial Rome, in opposition to pagan polytheism, the Jewish monotheistic tradition, and the many different teachings of Hellenistic philosophical and religious sects, the Christian religion was for a long period taught and practised in communities without any outward marks or symbols. The first Christian thinkers were entirely preoccupied with the spiritual nature of their faith. In the Mediterranean world, where strong artistic traditions stimulated the creative powers of talented artists, Christians long resisted the customs of their environment. The writer Tertullian, a Christian from North Africa living in the late second and early third centuries, mentions a painter who was converted to Christianity and henceforth was obliged to find another way of earning his living. Other writings testify that artists could not be accepted into the faith unless they renounced the making of any idols, since this profession was seen as a threat to the new religion. Christian theologians of the first half of the third century – Origen of Alexandria and Methodius, bishop of Olympus in Lycia – stressed that the worship of their God required neither temple, altar nor statue. Clement of Alexandria, a celebrated Christian writer of the late second and early third centuries, strongly opposed the pictorial representation of the Christian God, for his true image was *Logos* (the Word).

Learned theologians favoured an abstract conception of God confined to the domain of ideas, denying any possibility of his representation and apprehension by means of the senses. But less educated believers deviated from the strict conception of the learned. The Apocryphal Acts of the Apostles contains an interesting story of the portrait of the Apostle John which was painted in secret and then taken by his disciple Lycomedes to his room, where he placed it on an altar, adorned it with garlands and lit candles before it. The apostle rebuked his disciple for this, considering it to be childish behaviour, but Lycomedes kept the picture and, according to the custom of the times, showed his gratitude to his benefactor by thus honouring his portrait. This second-century legend originated in Asia Minor, where it was customary for the respect accorded a living person to be paid to his portrait as well. The Life of St Pancras, martyred in 304, contains a revealing description by one of his followers. "I ordered a portrait of my teacher, and when I gaze at his beloved face, I feel I am with him in person." Whether to honour a benefactor or to preserve the presence of the departed, Christians began to make use of painted images.

From the beginning of the third century, monuments marking graves of Christians steadily increased in number. Wall paintings in catacombs, reliefs on sarcophagi, and even sculptures in the round illustrated Old and New Testament teachings on the salvation of believers. However, even when they gradually adopted the traditional pictorial idiom of pagan art in order to convey the teachings of the Holy Scriptures, or when they used objects or figures (fish, ship, vine, Good Shepherd, praying figure, etc.) to allude to Christ, and even when they depicted Christ himself, these early Christian figural representations were not holy pictures venerated in particular places but didactic symbols, illustrations of salvation, redemption, and the life in Christ's kingdom promised to the faithful after death. The earliest pictures of Christ served to remind individuals, rather than the Church, of the long-vanished founder of the new faith.

When Emperor Constantine the Great (311–337) took Christianity as the established state religion in 313, the Church was obliged to make fundamental changes in its attitude to art. In response to the new circumstances, recognizing the Roman custom of emperor worship and the need for public observance of Christian ceremonies, the official Church inevitably accepted the role of art in Christian life. From that time, art dedicated to the imperial cult and that serving the glorification of Christ developed in parallel. From the early fourth century on, building and the arts, especially painting, served the Church's efforts to gather and teach the faithful, and convert the heathen. Constantine the Great and other powerful patrons raised imposing buildings on the sites where Christ and his followers died, decorated with paintings, reliefs and various church furnishings. This led to the creation of cult centres that attracted numerous pilgrims. Reliquaries and various objects that had come into contact with the relics of saints or fragments of the True Cross were taken from these places as highly-prized means of healing the sick and working various miracles. It was only a few learned men who regarded holy relics simply as objects capable of exciting religious fervour. In a funeral address for the martyr Theodore, Gregory, the celebrated writer and bishop of Nyssa in Asia Minor (d.394),

described those who experienced happiness merely by touching the relics: "... they put their eyes, lips, ears and all their senses into that act and thus, shedding tears of gratitude and passion, implored the martyr to intercede for them, as though he were alive and well in their midst." The bishop of Nyssa fully understood the need of the faithful for sensual impressions and to conjure up in their imaginations the holy personage to whom they applied for help. Sensual perception of a witness of Christ's divine powers, a martyr (Greek, *martyria* = testimony, bearing witness), whose sufferings were perpetuated in the minds of the faithful by means of his relics, offered a more effective way of strengthening Christian belief. The importance of the sensual appreciation of certain relics, emphasized in Christian writings of the late fourth century, paved the way for the acceptance of religious paintings that would recall the subject and evoke respect for his or her person.

Judging by legends and Lives of saints, it would seem that pictures of Christ and the saints were mostly regarded by the common people as objects themselves imbued with supernatural powers. Portraits of martyrs and stylites were attributed such powers at a very early date. The faithful used them as magical objects capable of defending them from evil. The church historian Theodoret of Antioch (d.466) mentions that in Rome the portrait of St Symeon the Stylite was painted over the entrance to many artisans' shops as their protector. Superstitions and traditional beliefs rooted in bygone pagan times attached themselves to various articles brought from holy places. Thus it came to be widely held that the saints continued to exercise their powers through their relics and portraits. The Church tacitly approved the didactic use of pictures showing New Testament figures and events, Christ's miracles or the Old Testament prophets who foretold Christ's coming, permitting such pictures on the walls of religious buildings. Nor did it attempt to suppress stories of the miraculous powers of relics or pictures brought from cult centres. In short, the Church allowed both the didactic and cult role of the painting, but for a long time refrained from clarifying its view on the true purpose of an image. The Council of Elvira (now Granada) in Spain, held in the first decade of the third century, had prohibited paintings in churches, but this decision seems to have had only a limited effect in a small area. In the East, the celebrated Cappadocian Fathers of the Church, Basil the Great (330–379), Gregory of Nyssa (d.394) and Gregory of Nazianzus (329/30–390), saw no danger of the early Christian works of art leading to idolatry. Some learned theologians even justified the role of images in fostering religious feeling. Asterius of Amasia in Pontus (late 4th c.), for instance, greatly admired the scenes of the martyrdom of St Euphemia painted in the martyrium dedicated to her; however, he was of the opinion that the person of Christ should not be depicted. The monk Nilus of Sinai, giving advice to a church founder, Prefect Olympiodorus, in the fifth century, declared that only Old and New Testament scenes should be painted in the church, in addition to a cross in the sanctuary. Since no mention is made of specially venerated icons among the church furnishings, it would seem probable that they were still not present in all churches at that time. From many written sources it appears that erudite bishops throughout the Eastern and Western Roman Empires particularly stressed the didactic role of paintings, since they could exert an influence on anyone who entered a place of worship. The mosaics commissioned by Pope Sixtus III (432–440) for the church of S. Maria Maggiore testify to the already customary method of decorating the interior walls of churches with scenes from the Holy Scriptures. The technique, skill and compositions of experienced Hellenistic artists were adopted for the execution of Christian works, so that a thread of anthropomorphic antique art was interwoven with the fabric of Christian artistic expression.

Persons from the Christian history were brought to life in pictures, arousing the admiration of those who supported their use or the resistance of stubborn traditionalists faithful to the original ideas of Christianity. In the course of this centuries-long conflict, the concept of the icon as a particularly venerated picture gradually took shape.

The famous church historian, Bishop Eusebius of Caesarea in Asia Minor (d.339), wrote a letter to Constantia, sister of Emperor Constantine the Great, refusing her request to procure for her an image of Christ with the admonition that God, although having two natures, divine and human, could not be depicted, since lifeless paint could not express the spiritual essence of the Word. Although this request had come from such an influential person, Eusebius remained true to his belief founded on abstract ideas. Endeavouring to explain to Constantia the abstract nature of God, he compared the deity with light: "How then could any person do the impossible? How could any man paint so wondrous and unattainable a form, if the term "form" is at all applicable to the divine and spiritual essence? Unless, in the manner of faithless pagans, one is to represent things that bear no possible resemblance to anything... Who, then, would be capable of producing the reflected shining beams of such exalted glory with soulless and lifeless paints and inanimate delineations?... Have you forgotten God's commandment forbidding the making of images either of what is in heaven or what is below on earth (Exod. XX, 4, Deut. V, 8)? Have you ever heard anything of the kind, either you yourself in church or from someone else, that any such thing has been spoken of in the Church? Has not all this been rejected all over the world and driven far from churches?..."

In the years when he was writing his *History of the Church,* Eusebius was aware, however, of many works of art depicting the cross as the symbol of Christianity or figures from Christian history. He knew of the statue of Christ and the woman ill of the flux in the town of Paneas (Caesarea in Palestine), of images of the Apostles Peter and Paul and of Christ; he knew that Emperor Constantine himself had commissioned the painting of the Prophet Daniel and the Good Shepherd (alluding to Christ) in the imperial palace in Constantinople; he was aware, too, that in a room of the palace the cross was displayed as the symbol of Christianity which had enabled the emperor to defeat Maxentius at the Battle of the Milvian Bridge, where, instead of earlier-won trophies signifying the presence of supernatural powers ensuring victory, Constantine the Great had held up the cross. During his campaigns, according to Eusebius, Constantine raised his tent, kept there the cross and prayed before it, awaiting divine inspiration and aid to give him victory. While not openly opposing the emperor's actions in the domain of art, and his introduction of pictures and symbols into court life to serve the imperial cult, Eusebius nevertheless remained a sceptical traditionalist, rejecting any possibility of representing Christ, even though he was endowed with a dual nature, since the divine nature must have altered the human.

Epiphanius of Salamina on Cyprus (d.403) was even more vehement in denouncing the custom of painting Christ, the Virgin Mary, martyrs, angels, apostles and prophets. "If images are accepted, heathen customs are at work," he declared, and on one occasion in a village church personally tore asunder a cloth on which Christ or a saint had been painted. Epiphanius even wrote a letter of protest to Emperor Theodosius II (379–395), a noted opponent of pagan cults, arguing that since artists depicted things they had never seen, their art was false. He therefore begged the emperor to ban the making of any mosaic representations of the apostles, prophets and Christ. Even in his will, in which he addressed his contemporaries, he reminded people that neither churches nor tombs of saints should be decorated with images.

Learned bishops of the time clearly affirmed that God could not be depicted by means of art, that an image, albeit Christian in subject, was necessarily false since it was not derived from anything visible, and might, moreover, encourage the spread of unforeseen forms of worshipping inanimate objects, as the people followed pagan customs. But none of this could check the ever more ramified development of the visual arts, which appears to have been approved by both the emperor and the Church establishment. What was still lacking, however, was a theological explanation of the difference between pagan idols and images of the Christian God represented in the same artistic media. Even so, the worship of Christ and the veneration of saints were spread for centuries precisely by the aid of images. Gradually, in the course of the fifth and sixth centuries, when the ancient disputes over the possibility of depicting Christ flared up in the form of heresies, and finally during the century of iconoclasm (726–843), the necessary theological interpretation was found, providing doctrinal justification of the existence and veneration of Christian icons.

In the early centuries of Christianity, many impulses unconnected with church teachings contributed to the cult of icons. A major role in this was played by popular belief in the supernatural power of relics or pictures of martyrs and stylites, but it is questionable whether such influences would have been sufficient had the Church not exploited them at various times. Seeking a theoretical basis for the pact between Church and State, as early as the fourth century emphasis was placed on the idea of Christ as the supreme ruler of the Christian universe, whose deputy on earth was the emperor of the Romaioi (as the Byzantine emperor was styled). Indeed, in the fourth century most of the known world around the Mediterranean was, in fact, under Byzantine sway. Eusebius of Caesarea speaks of Constantine the Great as the earthly ruler who owed his power to the Lord of the Heavens. The proclamation of Christ as the emperor of the Christian universe established a hierarchical system of power that enabled the emperor of the Romaioi to impose the idea of his absolute primacy on his subjects and neighbouring lands, and the bishops of the Christian Church to display images of Christ, according them the same honours as were paid to portraits of the temporal ruler.

Constantine the Great moved his capital from Rome to Byzantium on the Bosphorus in 330, and proclaimed that henceforth May 11 should be celebrated as the foundation date of the New Rome, which for the next millennium was to bear its founder's name – Constantinopolis. Until the sixth century, every May 11 the emperor's portrait was carried in a procession that formed part of the day's festivities. Moreover, the emperor's portraits are known to have been displayed on stands before which candles were lit as a mark of veneration, and accused persons fled to statues of the emperor seeking his protection and mercy. Any damage done to an imperial portrait was punished as though inflicted on the emperor's person. All these imperial cult practices, inherited from pagan times, continued to be respected in the Christian empire; it would certainly have been inconceivable to abolish them when the emperor adopted the Christian faith. On the contrary, his cult was still fostered and his image displayed, thus paving the way for the veneration of images of the divine ruler of the Christian universe. Even so, the practice of displaying icons of Christ grew very slowly, and was not equally popular in all periods and regions of the empire.

Philostorgius, another church historian, who lived in Constantinople in the first half of the fifth century, describes the burning of incense and candles, saying of prayers and the practice of apotropaic beliefs before the statue of Emperor Constantine the Great standing in the imperial forum in Constantinople. In the same texts he describes the statue of Christ in the city of Paneas in Palestine, but makes no mention of similar forms of worship in connection with it when he explains that it was removed from the city square to a local church during the reign of Julian the Apostate (361–363). It would seem that Christ's image was still not necessarily honoured everywhere in the same manner as the imperial portrait. The latter was displayed in courts of law, market-places, theatres, assembly halls, in fact, in all public places, both as a substitute for the emperor, and to signify his approval of the acts of his representatives. When a new emperor came to the throne, his portrait was sent to all the provinces of the vast empire, so that his subjects could swear allegiance to him. Any refusal to accord the portrait all the customary honours implied refusal to recognize the new ruler, and resulted in armed conflict. Severian of Gaballa in Syria (d. after 408) states explicitly: "The image of the emperor replaces him when he is absent... and the people revere it, honouring not the image but the person of the emperor."

Severian's explanation that the attitude to the picture is to be understood as the attitude to the person portrayed, i.e. that the image should be conceived as the intermediary between the viewer and the person honoured, was extremely important in the development of Christian ideas, since theologians adopted this line of thought when later seeking to explain the attitude towards the painted image of Christ, and to Christ as God made manifest in human form. The famous Cappadocian theologian Basil the Great (d.379) declared that "the honour accorded the image belongs to the original model", but for a long time this idea expressed in reference to the emperor's portrait was not applied to the interpretation of Christ's image in the form of an icon. On the contrary, throughout the fifth century most writers stressed the magical might of Christ's image, believing it to possess supernatural power. Rufinus of Aquileia, a writer who died in 410, also left a description of Christ's statue in Paneas, but unlike Eusebius and Philostorgius, he mentions the story of a plant possessing miraculous healing powers since it grew near Christ's figure. Rufinus simply reports the deep-seated popular belief that contact with the image of the deity worked miracles. Christ likewise appeared in visions to perform the unexpected. According to Zacharias, bishop of Mitylene (d.553), whose account is preserved in a Syrian chronicle, even the King of Persia, Kavadh, had one such vision: on capturing the city of Amida on the Tigris from the Byzantines in 504, the King came upon an icon of Christ in the treasury of a local church, and declared on that occasion that he had already seen it, for Christ had appeared to him and foretold his victory.

In writings from the second half of the sixth century there is a rapid increase in the number of legends about miracle-working icons of Christ and the Virgin Mary, and of reports of veneration of icons. Pagan beliefs and superstitions and many old customs were grafted onto the new cults. From the works of St Augustine (5th c.), who was opposed to the depiction of the divinity, we learn that a certain Marcellina worshipped Christ, St Paul, Homer and Pythagoras, burning incense before their images. In the sixth and seventh centuries, reports by writers and pilgrims on the burning of incense are ever more numerous; clearly the ancient customs and forms of worship were repeated before the icons of Christ, the Virgin Mary and the saints. Anthony of Piacenza described, in about 570, how he genuflected in Pilate's Praetorium in Jerusalem before an image of Christ, and in Memphis (Egypt) before the first image of Christ's face: the cloth, in fact, used by Christ to wipe himself, on which the imprint of his visage was preserved: *palium lineum in quo est effigies Salvatoris* (the linen cloth on which is the image of the Saviour). At about the same time, the legend arose in Edessa (on the Tigris) of the existence of Christ's picture not made by human hand, which Christ himself presented to Emperor Abagar. According to the writings of Ebagrius Scholasticus (d.600), this image saved Edessa during the Persian siege of 544. The legend of Emperor Abagar had been recounted earlier by Eusebius of Caesarea and Procopius (6th c.), but Ebagrius was the first to describe Christ's image as an apotropaic symbol "not made by human hand" *(archeiropoietos).* Learned bishops at the end of the sixth century were clearly in need of a fresh explanation to account for the image as the vehicle of God's will, or the picture possessing supernatural power. Such pictures would have to be ascribed a supernatural origin. Various explanations were put forward in the form of legends, but the most successful were those about icons of Christ and the Mother of God which, it was believed, were not made by human hand but resulted from direct contact with the holy persons. The pilgrim Theodosius went in the sixth century to pray to the figure and face of Christ impressed on the pillar on which he was scourged in Jerusalem. The same impression was later mentioned by Anthony of Piacenza, indicating that this relic, which was at the same time an image, attracted great attention among the faithful. Palestine, naturally, abounded in holy places, relics, and miraculous images, but major cities and monasteries extant elsewhere also enhanced their prestige by procuring similar rareties. Theodorus Lector writes around 530 that Eudocia, wife of Emperor Theodosius II, when in Jerusalem, sent the portrait of the Mother of God, painted by the Evangelist Luke, to Pulcheria (daughter of Emperor Arcadius), who lived in Constantinople until 453. Similar icons believed to be true portraits and to have been touched by the holy personage were of particular importance. The need for such icons steadily increased in the course of the sixth century, especially in the reign of Justinian I (527–565), marked by intensive church-building throughout the vast reunited empire. In this period stories of the self-reproduction of these authentic icons were very effective, especially when a narrating responded to the need of a faithful to recognize the face of God by means of senses. "How can I worship him when he is invisible and I do not know him?" asks a woman in a Syrian chronicle. Her wish was answered: she found an image of Christ imprinted on a linen cloth in her well, and when she wrapped this miraculous picture in her own scarf, the image produced its own copy, described in the story as *archeiropoietos.* To protect the icon, a church was built in the town of Camuliana (Asia Minor): the icon continued to multiply, one of its copies being carried in procession through the cities of Asia Minor between 554 and 560 to collect funds for rebuilding some ruined churches. To justify using this icon for such a practical purpose, the chronicler directs the reader's attention to the parallel between the arrival of an icon in a city and "Christ's Second Coming into this world", though all the details of the ceremonial described recall, in fact, the welcome and arrival *(Adventus)* of a victorious emperor returning from a campaign.

Like the bishops, emperors and generals learnt early on to exploit popular belief in the miraculous power of images. This was undoubtedly one of the main reasons that both the emperors and the Church ascribed great power to the icons of Christ and the Mother of God. The Byzantine chronicler Theophilactus Simocates (early 7th c.) records that as early as the year 586 in a battle against the Persians, on the river Arzamon, the general, in order to encourage Philippicus and his men, raised an icon of Christ "not made by human hand". Somewhat later, Emperor Heraclius (610–644) made use of a similar icon of Christ (probably the one from Camuliana or a copy of it which Emperor Justin II had brought to Constantinople in 574), bearing it as a protective insignia in his campaign against the Persians, according to George Pisides, an early seventh- century Byzantine poet. The display of an icon whose miraculous power was well known among the populace was an oft-repeated and effective means of raising morale. During the defence of Constantinople in 626, when the Persians were close to the city and it was being attacked from the landward side by Avars, Slavs, Bulgars and other "barbarians", the most venerated icons in the city were brought out. Theodore Syncellus, an eye-witness, recounted that during the siege Patriarch Sergius I (610–638) gave orders that as soon as night fell the Virgin with Christ was to be painted on all the gates on the western side of the city walls. Later, when the city was set on fire, the patriarch himself carried a miracle-working icon of Christ around the walls, praying continuously to strengthen the defenders' resistance. This same event was recorded by another contemporary, George

Pisides. The use of icons to inspire the common people, whose aid was essential at critical moments of a war, was repeated during later sieges, for example in 717–718, when Constantinople was attacked by the Arabs, but on this occasion it was an icon of the Virgin that was carried round the city walls in procession, together with a fragment of the True Cross. Just as Roman emperors had formerly displayed their trophies before their legions as symbols of victory won with the aid of the gods who favoured the emperor, so the Christian rulers of the Byzantine Empire, the patriarchs and bishops displayed the cross and icons, signifying triumph granted by the will of Christ. The general belief in the divine origin of the ruler's victorious power was exploited by Byzantium, as it had been in the Roman Empire, as an infallible means of securing political power. This is why the existence and veneration of icons more and more assumed an official character, and the portable icon was increasingly evident in public life in times of war and peace, in churches and at the court. The honours previously accorded only to the emperor's portrait were increasingly apparent in the worship of Christ's image. Not only in Constantinople and the eastern provinces but in Rome, too, the icon of Christ "not made by hand" was carried in processions.

From the mid-sixth until the early eighth century, icons of Christ are mentioned more and more often in written sources. In the time of Justinian I, the great champion of the conversion to Christianity of the restored empire, which stretched from Cordoba and Gibraltar to the Tigris and the Euphrates, from the Alps and the Danube to the Nile, the icon was given, it seems, a specific place in the church. Justinian completely rebuilt the church of St Sophia in Constantinople and gave artists the opportunity to express Christian ideas on the altar screen, on which the most important icons were placed. When the Athenian Academy, where pagan scholars, the Neo-Platonists, had taught, was closed down at Justinian's behest in 529, the last resistance of ancient Greek philosophy was officially removed. However, in the restored empire, Christian doctrinal conflicts, which had already emerged at ecumenical councils in the fourth and fifth centuries, caused increasing upheavals in both Church and State. The dispute concerning the divine and human natures of Christ, which none of Justinian's councils was able to solve, reflected political differences, or rather the separatist aspirations of certain parts of the empire and major sees – Rome, Alexandria and Antioch, which were steadfastly opposed by the central authorities, striving to secure primacy for the patriarch of Constantinople. The decision of the Council of Chalcedon (451) on the dual "indivisible but separate" natures of Christ was not the only source of dispute. The primacy of the pope of Rome was acknowledged, but the equal rights accorded the bishops of Old and New Rome later led to a steady deterioration in their relations, even though Rome had accepted the Chalcedon decree. Rejecting this and affirming their belief in the single divine nature (Greek, *physis*) of God, the Monophysites of Syria, Egypt and Armenia stubbornly pursued a policy contrary to the interests of the central Byzantine authorities.

The Byzantine emperors were personally involved in all church disputes, keeping an eye on their political consequences and safeguarding the absolutist character of imperial rule. The policy adopted by the emperor and his attitude to church dogma had repercussions on art, particularly in the domain of icons. Scholars have noted that the oldest stories of icons of Christ "not made by hand" date from the second half of the sixth century, and that observation indicates precisely the reason why they originated in the period when intense efforts were being made to win over the representatives of the eastern provinces, where Persian incursions and heresies were weakening central control. Such icons worked miracles in Camuliana, Edessa, Amida and Memphis, i.e. precisely in the regions where it was most necessary to affirm Constantinople's view that it was possible to represent Christ, the Word made Man. Patriarch Sergius I and Emperor Heraclius made various attempts to find interpretations of doctrine that would satisfy Constantinople, Rome and the eastern provinces. They first put forward the theory of the two natures but single divine energy of Christ. As this did not prove effective, Patriarch Sergius I proposed a new teaching that Christ had two natures but one divine will (Greek, *thelema*). This Monothelite doctrine was accepted by Emperor Heraclius himself, and a new church edict was posted in the narthex of St Sophia's in Constantinople in 638. But this attempt to unite the Church also failed: Rome rejected the imperial edict and the Arabs conquered the eastern provinces. In the times when Byzantine rulers were suffering ever more frequent military defeats and the empire's territory was appreciably reduced, the emperors of the Romaioi, as the Byzantine rulers designated themselves, laid ever greater stress on their fidelity to Christ, and even on their subservience. The Arabs overran Mesopotamia, Armenia and the Dvin region (640), Cappadocia and Caesarea (647), Egypt and Alexandria (646), and then Cyprus, Rhodes and Kos. From the sixth century, Avars, Slavs, Bulgars and other peoples penetrated into the Balkans; by 711 the whole of North Africa was under Arab rule. It was precisely in this period that the divine origin of the power of the Byzantine emperors·was increasingly emphasized. No longer having any control over much of his formerly vast realms, the emperor placed even greater stress on the mystical origin of his authority, thereby defending his position as Christ's sole regent on earth. Since the glorification of Christ suited the state ideology of Byzantium in this period, it may be assumed that the state encouraged the spread of the cult of Christ's icons.

Christ's image is impressed on the coins of Justinian II (685–695 and 705–711): Christ is designated *Rex Regnantium,* while Justinian II, depicted on the reverse, is termed *servus Christi.* In this age, when the Church of Constantinople was giving increasing support to the cult of Christ's image, opposition to Constantinople and to icons was steadily growing in the eastern provinces. The influence of the teachings of the Jews and the Arabs, who were against any anthropomorphic representations in their places of worship, helped to exacerbate the dispute over icons. At the end of the seventh century, monks in Armenia waged a fierce struggle against pictures in churches. In response to their attacks, an apologia was published declaring that "we apprehend the invisible through what is visible". Finally, the Church spoke out officially in defence of icons and anthropomorphic representations of Christ: at the V/VI Council, held in Constantinople in 692, it was decreed that artists should not depict John the Baptist pointing to a lamb, but in future should paint Christ in human form, since this would remind the faithful of his passion, death and the possibility of redemption for mankind.

The representation of God in anthropomorphic form, a principle of classical art, was then officially accepted in the Christian world, but only in the east European regions: Rome did not respect it, while the near-eastern provinces stoutly defended the view that the abstract essence of God could not be expressed by the icon. The ideological conflict between East and West was violently manifested in the eighth century with the brutal destruction of works of art.

It is interesting to note, however, that even before the great iconoclast crisis (726–843), it was not unknown in Byzantium for pictures to be destroyed if they were not in accordance with current doctrinal teachings. When the supporters of Arianism broke with the Church, they burnt statues of the patriarch and a picture of the Virgin with Christ at Milion in Constantinople (in the reign of Constantius, 337–361); when Emperor Anastasius I (491–518) adopted the Monophysite position, he brought to the capital a Syrian artist, a follower of the Manichaean faith, who painted works in the imperial palace and St Stephen's church which differed completely from the customary manner of representing Christ, and caused a popular revolt; when Emperor Bardanes Philippicus (711–713), an Armenian, reinstated Monophysite teaching as the only valid doctrine of the Byzantine Church, thereby steering state policy towards the eastern provinces, he destroyed a picture of the VI Ecumenical Council (680–681) in the imperial palace, since this gathering had condemned the Monothelite view; he also removed the inscription on the Milion Gate mentioning this council, and returned to their places portraits of Patriarchs Sergius I and Honorius, adherents of the doctrine he himself had adopted. Opposing Emperor Philippicus, Pope Constantine I proclaimed his views in Rome in similar fashion: he refused to accept the portrait of the new, heretical, emperor, no coins with his image were struck in Rome, and his name was not mentioned in church services. As an even clearer sign of his rejection of Philippicus' Monothelite policy, Pope Constantine I ordered pictures of all six ecumenical councils to be painted in St Peter's.

The displaying or removing of images as a symbolic method of indicating doctrinal or political views was thus a centuries-old custom among the Byzantines. The same means was adopted by Emperor Leo III (717–741) to assert a new political and doctrinal course. By glorifying himself as emperor and high priest, he endeavoured to wean the populace from the veneration of holy icons, and ordered the removal of Christ's image from the bronze gates (Chalke) of the imperial palace. This act, however, set off rioting in the streets of the capital and aroused fierce opposition, showing that the honouring of icons had already become deeply entrenched in the minds of the people. The patriarch of Constantinople, the pope and the European part of the empire resolutely opposed this policy of Leo III, who was regarded by his contemporaries as an admirer of Arab culture. The emperor's open denunciation of icons in 726, and an official edict against them issued in 730, marked the start of a century and more of bloodshed in the struggles between the state and church authorities, between the iconoclasts and iconophiles, between the eastern and European policies in the empire. The initial conflict between the emperor and patriarch later spread to all sections of society, and prompted learned men on both sides to rise in defence of their beliefs.

The earlier teachings of Philostorgius and Pseudo-Dionysius the Areopagite (1st c.) on the essence of the image and its relationship to its prototype assumed broader significance only in the eighth century, when they were put forward by the defenders of icons. Philostorgius and, even more clearly, Pseudo-Dionysius had presented the Christian interpretation of Neo-Platonists' ideas of the Greek and Roman philosophers; on the physical and spiritual worlds as parts of a general hierarchical order, the world of the senses as a reflection of the world of the spirit, the contemplation of symbols, comprehensible to the senses, which allow an ascent towards the spiritual. According to Pseudo-Dionysius, through visible images the spirit can attain a perception of the divine, i.e. reach the spiritual through the sensual *(dia tōn aisthetōn epi ta noe)* and from symbols representing what is sacred can aspire to the heights of the heavenly hierarchy. It seems that not much attention was paid to these explanations, which were to gain lasting acceptance in later centuries, at the time when they were propounded. Nor did the words of John of Damascus (c. 675–c. 749), who was the first to grasp the full gravity of the conflict of eastern and western traditions regarding imagery, have much impact at the beginning, for Damascus lived outside the Byzantine frontiers, in Palestine, which was already under the rule of an Arab caliph. The representative of Christians at the court of Sargun Ibn Mansoor in Damascus, and later a monk in the monastery of St Sabbas of Jerusalem near Jerusalem, John of Damascus finally put into context in 726–730 the essential significance of imagery in relation to Christian doctrine: "The image is a resemblance, an example of something that is revealed... Certainly the image is not in every respect similar to the prototype, i.e. to the subject represented, for a picture is one thing and that which the artist wishes to depict another, and there are bound to be differences between them... For example, the picture of a man shows his bodily features, but it is not endowed with his spiritual qualities..." Answering the question as to the purpose of a picture, Damascus writes: "Every image depicts something that is hidden. By this I mean the following: since a man cannot directly perceive the invisible (the spirit being concealed by the body), since he lacks the power to see into the future, or what is separated and distant from him in space, since he is confined in both place and time, the picture has been devised to indicate the path to knowledge and reveal what is hidden..."

Respecting neither the arguments of the defenders of the icon nor the beauty of works of art, Leo III ordered icons to be brought from all churches and homes to a square in Constantinople, where they were burnt. In the persecutions and punishments that followed, human life was taken. The iconoclast council held at Hieria near Constantinople in 754, in which Emperor Constantine V participated, forbade the representation of God the Word in any pictorial form. The pope and the eastern patriarchs did not attend this council. In 751, the Byzantine Exarchate of Ravenna had fallen under Langobard control, and the pope had proposed an alliance to Pipin, king of the Franks, thereby separating himself from Byzantium. Thus, the iconophile policy of the pope enabled artistic activity to continue normally throughout the iconoclast crisis in the East.

During the reign of Empress Irene and her minor son, Constantine VI, an iconophile council was held in Nicaea (787) and the cult of icons was temporarily restored. The defenders of the icon decided at this council that "...revered and holy images, whether wall paintings or made of mosaic or any other suitable material, should be displayed in God's churches, on holy vessels and church vestments, on walls and wood panels, in homes and at the roadside – both the image of our Lord and Saviour, Jesus Christ, and those of the immaculate Virgin, the Mother of God, of the holy angels, all the saints and the righteous. Indeed, the more often these painted images are seen, the more those who observe them will call to mind the originals, turn to them, bear witness to them, kissing them as worthy of veneration, but this is not the usual worship,... for the veneration accorded an image is directed upward to the original."

This explanation formed the basis of the teachings of the iconophiles and of later supporters of Patriarch Methodius, the minor Emperor Michael III, and his mother, Theodora, who officially proclaimed the establishment of the cult of icons in 843.

Few icons have been preserved from this early period of Christian art, and these mostly in regions far from Constantinople where the iconophiles had greater influence: in Rome, in the Coptic monasteries of Egypt, at Sinai, and in Georgia, which adopted Christianity as early as the 4th century. The oldest surviving icons are considered to date from the 6th or 7th century. They depict Christ, the Mother of God, apostles and saints. Christ and the first witnesses to his divine powers are represented on 6th-century icons with established physical features and holding certain objects, such as a Gospel, cross or scroll; they are identified by a nimbus and shown only in certain poses. As they stand or sit with a serene composure, their huge eyes gaze fixedly at the observer. All these figures are depicted as denizens of a realm beyond time and space; they show no emotions, play no part in earthly life, do not move, impart instruction or suffer. Only their expressive eyes, always considered a mirror of the soul, suggest the artist's desire to approach eternity, God. While portraits of the saints and martyrs might conceivably have provided the basis for the creation of their standard iconographic images, in the case of Christ, the Mother of God and the apostles the physical form was sought in doctrinal ideas and in tradition. The earliest representations of Christ are known to have varied: some showed him young, others old; some ascribed to him the appearance of Zeus, while others showed him as a Greek philosopher. In the icons of the 6th century, he was mainly depicted as the *Pantocrator,* the lord of the Christian universe and saviour of mankind, a middle-aged man with a calm, austere and thoughtful countenance. A 6th-century Coptic icon painted in tempera on wood (now in the Louvre) shows Christ as *Psôtir* (sic! Saviour), while St Menas beside Christ is described as a supplicant, interceding for the faithful before Christ the Saviour (APA MENA PROEISTOS). The reduced bodily forms, the insignificant bodies with large heads and huge eyes, the quiet ochre and olive-green tones of this picture, reflect the typical oriental tendency towards the abstract and disregard for all the canons of beauty upheld by the Greeks and Romans, both pagan and Christian, in the early centuries after Christ.

The classical conception of beauty is believed to have survived longest in the icons originating in Constantinople. Several in this style have been preserved in the monastery of St Catherine on Mount Sinai, while some of these oldest icons were taken in the 19th century to Berlin and Russia (now in Kiev). They were executed in encaustic, an ancient technique of mixing paint with hot wax employed by Mediterranean artists. In one such icon St John the Baptist, holding a scroll with an inscription (John I, 29), stands like a Greek philosopher, an orator, resting the weight of his body on one leg, and points with a sweeping gesture towards Christ in a medallion. Opposite Christ in another medallion is the Mother of God (resembling the *imagines clipeatae* of the emperor and empress in a consular diptych). The icon thus conveys the idea of Christ's human and divine natures, and the intercession of St John and the Virgin for the salvation of mankind. Vigorous brush-strokes and dense colours clearly define the contours of the prophet's body beneath the folds of his rough dark-coloured robes. His large expressive eyes, full lips framed in his thick moustache and beard, and long flowing robes make a strong impact on the observer. The impression of relief achieved by the use of colour reveals a classical conception of the beauty of the human body and a painter acquainted with both the technique and stylistic canons of Greco-Roman artists.

The same treatment of the human form, albeit executed in lighter and more vivid colours, is to be found in the icon of the Virgin with Christ, likewise in Kiev, and that of St Peter in the Sinai collection, which also contains a famous Virgin with Christ, saints and angels, and one of the most beautiful encaustic icons, a bust of Christ with the Gospels (Pantocrator). None of these encaustic icons is now kept in its original place, so that their actual purpose is not known – whether they were intended for collective veneration in church or for private religious observances in homes or monastic cells. Some are fairly large, others quite small. All of them, however, like the famous encaustic icon of SS Sergius and Bacchus also in Kiev (6th c.), testify to an already established iconography, to a specified manner of representing the appearance of figures from Christian history and their mutual relationships, and to the benefits and aid that Christians expected to receive from icons. The role of intermediary accorded them by the faithful is already apparent in the icons of saints. Seeking salvation, they addressed Christ through the Virgin, John the Baptist, martyrs and saints. This is why in these "Constantinopolitan icons" the saint intercessor is usually depicted full-length, as a person who is present, while Christ is only in a medallion, as a portrait of one who is absent, an *imago clipeata,* in the same way as the absent emperor is depicted with the present consul in ivory diptychs. Byzantine imperial iconography and classical treatment of the figures are characteristic of these oldest Constantinopolitan icons.

Roman icons of the 6th and 7th centuries already display certain features that were to be fully developed in west European painting in the Middle Ages. Very early on the Roman Church represented the Virgin Mary as an empress. In the encaustic icon preserved in the church of St Mary in the Roman quarter of Trastevere (La Madonna della Clemenza), the Virgin wears a jewel-encrusted crown with pendants and a purple dalmatic with an ornamented collar, and holds a cruciform sceptre. Seated on a throne with the infant Christ on her lap, she is guarded by two angels, like the Empress of Heaven. The combination of stiffness and movement, of the ceremonial solemnity of the Virgin's attire and the vivid colours of the angels' robes, of the rigid figure of the empress and the strong contours of the angels' regular features, their heads turned towards her – all this marks a new style emerging from the neglected vestiges of classical painting. Different qualities are evident, however, in some icons of the Sinai collection which are considered to have originated in Palestine: the absence of any three-dimensionality and reduction of form to the surface, the pronounced line, and lack of any impression of depth or space set apart the diptych icon of the equestrian saints, George and Theodore. The lack of information on the artists and provenance of these and many other icons calls for caution and restraint in drawing conclusions on the part of scholars and art connoisseurs. It is evident, though, that these portable holy pictures were produced in numerous workshops in monasteries and at the imperial court. Icons travelled from one end of the empire to the other as precious gifts, as indispensable objects before which individuals professed their faith or prayed for mercy and salvation, as miracle-working symbols of the power of those who possessed them.

For prominent individuals, small icons, often in the form of diptychs, triptychs or polyptychs, were made of ivory, silver, gold, enamel, steatite, bone or wood. Few of these are left from the early period of Byzantine art, but the most costly are thought to have originated in Constantinople. In the distant Caucasus regions, however, a huge treasury of this art has been preserved, enabling us to imagine all the brilliance and beauty of workmanship of the earliest icons. The icons with silver sheathing (revêtement) and frames dating from the 9th to 12th centuries are of particular importance. There are also sections of altar screens from the 9th, 10th, 11th and later centuries, and masonry altar screens from the 11th century. Remarkable for their size and workmanship are the silver and silver-gilt crosses which stood before the altar in Georgian churches, reflecting the light from the high windows below the dome. The classical art of hammering figures on silver leaf, which was then affixed to a wooden base, was used by experienced Caucasian craftsmen in the making of icons and crosses. The wealth of donors and commissioners of works of art intended for the decoration of churches or homes kept alive this artistic craft for centuries. The long continuity of artistic endeavour to depict the stories of Christian saints and Christ on silver plaques, employing eastern Christian iconography and long-established compositions, led to the exceptional precision of workmanship and beauty of form displayed by icons from the 11th and 12th centuries. The Caucasian masters were inspired not only by the generally recognized Christian saints but also by local cults. St George, for instance, was very frequently depicted as a knight on horseback (as in other Christian lands), and also, in accordance with Georgian legend, as the slayer of Emperor Diocletian, shown pierced by the saint's lance and trampled under his horse's hooves. In Georgia, Diocletian was a symbol of evil, the embodiment of the enemies of Christianity, who was overthrown by the celebrated holy warrior. Many other specific features are present in the icons of the Caucasian regions from the 9th, 10th and 11th centuries, and even down to the 18th, when the glorious tradition of the religious art of the educated was submerged in folk art.

Respecting the fundamental canons of eastern Christian art, the Georgian masters adopted the traditional compositions and basic iconographic rules, but introduced stylistic features that clearly diverged from Constantinopolitan trends. The highly stylized lines of the shallow folds of drapery and the clean flowing lines of the contours of the figures, most frequently Christ and the Virgin, emphasize the symmetry of the composition and convey a serene, exalted and dignified impression. Disregard for anatomical form, which is subordinated to geometrical stylization, gives the figures a majestic monumentality even in the icons of small size in churches at Chukuli, Chihareshi, Djahunderi, etc. The 10th-century silver icons from churches in Paki, Gelati, Lagurka and Martvili exemplify the distinctive style developed in the extensive Caucasian regions.

As early as the 10th century, artists in Georgia often signed their work. Their fame spread and they were very early on regarded as valued members of society, whose work was highly esteemed and well rewarded. In the late 10th and early 11th centuries, contacts between Georgia and Byzantium led to more intensive artistic exchanges and to the more frequent adoption of Constantinopolitan conceptions of the icon. This occurred again in the 12th and then in the 14th century, when patrons of art and artists once more paid closer attention to events in the Byzantine capital. The Georgian Orthodox Church adopted the decisions of the patriarchate of Constantinople on forms of worship, and continued to decorate the altar screen in accordance with the Constantinopolitan tradition. In Armenia, however, the Monophysite doctrine prevailed: the icon and the decorated altar screen disappeared from churches, and the activity of church benefactors was mostly confined to commissioning illuminated manuscripts. The works of art of the Caucasian lands, and above all of Georgia, where the demand for costly icons for centuries attracted the most talented artists, provide contemporary scholars and art lovers with an insight into the world of those Christian artists who were equally versed in the ideas of East and West, Persia and Byzantium, the Christian art of Palestine and of Constantinople.

Our knowledge of the oldest Constantinopolitan icons and altar screens is partly augmented by written sources. The verses of Paul Silentiarius read in St Sophia's in Constantinople in 563 conjure up the vision of gleaming icons on the altar screen of the capital's most important church, and convey, albeit in imprecise poetic terms, a powerful impression of the beauty of this costly screen separating the nave from the altar. Twelve columns supported the architrave and were connected by closure slabs, and three doors giving access to the altar. The entire screen, both the closure slabs in the lower part and the columns and architrave above, were covered with silver, its reflected light illuminating a wide area around. The architrave had medallions engraved with images of Christ, the Virgin, angels, apostles and prophets, while on the central slabs of the altar screen the artist depicted, also in medallions, the cross and the monograms of the emperor and empress – the founder Justinian I and his consort Theodora. Nothing except this description has survived of this magnificent screen separating the nave (naos), intended for the congregation, and the sanctuary, accessible only to the clergy. On this screen, symbolizing the division of the material and spiritual, the temporal and heavenly kingdoms, artists conveyed, as early as the 6th century, the essential ideas of Christian teaching – the possibility of the salvation of the faithful, and intercession on their behalf before the Judge and Saviour by St John (probably shown among the prophets) and the Virgin Mary. The figures of the prophets who foretold Christ's kingdom and the apostles who preached it appear at a very early date on the screen that led the faithful into the mystic world of the promised heavenly kingdom. The figures in medallions carved on the architrave of the altar screen, as described by this high official and poet of Justinian I, seem to explain precisely these fundamental ideas of Christian teaching. Similar altar screens of stone, metal, ceramics, brick or wood preserved in other 6th-century and later churches testify to the generosity and wealth of the founders. But regardless of the intrinsic value of the materials used, all the forms and decorative elements carried the same message: the possibility of attaining the heavenly kingdom ruled by Christ Pantocrator, to whom the Virgin and St John intercede on behalf of the faithful.

All Byzantine Greek churches and those of other Orthodox nations had their altar screen. Many are preserved, but an even greater number has been destroyed, so that our knowledge of the development of the altar screen is still incomplete and imprecise. It is known that 4th-century churches had a very low screen, scarcely more than knee-height, enabling the congregation to follow the liturgy in full. In time, the height of the screen gradually increased in the East, and in the post-Byzantine period completely concealed the altar region from laymen. Gradually, in the course of the 18th and 19th centuries, decoration vanished from the church walls and was concentrated on the altar screen, now called the iconostasis, which became the only place for paintings and reliefs in the interior of Orthodox churches.

The number of icons on altar screens and their range of subjects began to increase in the Middle Ages. The interruption in the evolution of symbolic pictorial representation caused by disputes over the icon had its repercussions even after the Triumph of Orthodoxy (843) in many provinces of the empire, in consequence of the renewed efforts by Paulicians, Monophysites and others to re-establish the state of affairs under the iconoclast emperors (Leo III, Constantine V, Leo IV, Leo V, Michael II and Theophilus). The removal of symbolic ornamentation from altar screens is recorded by an opponent of the iconoclasts, Patriarch Nicephorus (805–815), who mentions hangings, closure slabs, columns and doors of altar screens with representations of animals and monsters: "...for they serve merely to decorate and embellish". Such ornamentation was subsequently retained on the stone and wood closure slabs, capitals and architraves of altar screens in the 11th, 12th, 13th and later centuries, but it was the icons which then gave the screen its real purpose.

It is understandable that in a period of conflicts and upheavals, altar screen ornamentation was not uniform in all provinces of the empire. This was a matter decided by local bishops, in accordance with their own views. But regardless of whether icons appeared on altar screens earlier or later in a particular region, their acceptance entailed a certain range of subjects, in which the Deesis – the Virgin and St John interceding before Christ the Judge – occupied the central place. Whether the images were carved in the stone or metal of the architrave beam, painted on a templon (a wooden panel extending the length of the architrave) or took the form of individual icons arranged in a composition, in the earliest period they all depicted the same subject – the prayer of the holy intercessors. The "simple" Deesis composition with three figures might be extended by the addition of two angels, evangelists or a row of apostles (the Grand Deesis), and even the figure of a martyr or saint chosen by the church founder or donor of the altar screen as his personal protector and church patron. On the stone altar screens of the ninth and tenth centuries, the patrons of individuals and intercessors for mankind pray to Christ for the salvation of those under their protection. Very often these holy figures are depicted in medallions carved on the stone beam, but sometimes also in high relief set in very decorative arcades. In icons, the figures are always set in frames, either carved in relief, painted on the templon, or executed in mosaic or other material. The purpose of the frame was to set the icon apart as an individual venerated image with its own cult, regardless of whether it was placed on the altar screen or in some other part of the church.

From the post-iconoclast period records have been preserved of screens and icons made of a variety of materials. In the church of Christ the Saviour in Constantinople, Emperor Basil I raised a costly altar screen whose "columns and lower parts are made entirely of silver, while the architrave resting on the capitals is of pure gold, with all the treasures of India scattered on it. The image of our Lord God as man is represented several times in enamel on this beam..." This description seems to suggest that events from the Gospels were depicted at this early date on the architrave of Basil's altar screen even though only Christ, the most important participant in such events, is actually mentioned.

Other sources from the 10th century indicate the inclusion of another row of icons, scenes of the major church feasts, above or beside the Deesis on the architrave of the altar screen. In this period specially venerated icons were placed on either side of the screen, on the walls or the columns it rested against. These icons also had ornate frames, carved in relief or painted in fresco technique to imitate stone-carving. Their subjects were Christ and the Virgin or the Virgin with Child, and particularly revered saints. The imagery previously confined to the architrave thus spread onto the lateral walls and columns adjacent to the screen (as, for example, in the church of St Sophia in Nicaea, the Protaton on Mount Athos, the Panaghia in Phocis, all 10th c.). Only fragments have survived of some of the elaborate screens from this period. They include a 10th-century white marble slab with plaques inlaid with coloured stone, paste and glass (*opus Alexandrinum*), depicting St Eudocia from the Constantinopolitan church raised by an eminent imperial official, Constantine Lips, and a marble slab, part of a templon probably from c. 900, with three apostles executed in marble inlay and finished in encaustic technique, now in the Byzantine Museum in Athens.

Stone altar screens with figural ornamentation (the Deesis and the founder's patron saint) dating from the 11th century have been found in churches in Asia Minor (Sebaste, fragments in the museum in Afyonkarahisar) and southern Greece (Thebes, island of Chios), indicating that after 843 Constantinople again influenced the work of artists in the provinces that had been less opposed to the establishment of the cult of icons. If they lacked sufficient wealth and the skilled artists required for work in mosaic, enamel or marble inlay, donors in provincial towns and villages commissioned artists to paint fresco icons on the walls of churches. These pseudo-icons, no longer portable, were separated from the other wall paintings by ornate carved stone frames or painted imitations of these. For example, in St Sophia's in Ohrid (Macedonia, mid-11th c.), both columns which formerly flanked the original altar screen have fresco-icons of the Virgin with Christ, symbolically representing Holy Wisdom (Haghia Sophia) to which the church is dedicated. On the altar screen of the church at Nerezi near Skopje (1164), the contemporary icons that once occupied the spaces between the columns have vanished, but the huge fresco-icons of the Virgin with Christ and St Panteleimon have been preserved (the latter completely) on the columns at the ends of the screen. Marble was used for the columns and the architrave they support, and for the fresco-icon frames, richly carved by talented craftsmen working for a founder who was a member of the imperial family. In the cave church of St Neophytus on Cyprus (late 12th c.), however, wood was used for both the screen and the icons placed on it, which were periodically carried in processions. In the church of the Holy Archangels in the Georgian village of Yprari (1096), the cave church of St Sophia on Cythera (12th c.), and the so-called Evangelistria at Yeraki in the Peloponnese (second half of 12th c.), the altar screen was made of brick and painted with frescoes. Thanks to these surviving examples of masonry altar screens, we know that as early as the 11th century icons painted in fresco technique filled the spaces between the columns. Much of the church service took place behind the altar screen, both in the capital, and in remote lands which followed the Orthodox teachings imposed by Constantinople. Written sources record that Abbot Desiderius of Monte Cassino (1058–1086) obtained from Constantinople a templon with six silver columns and ten icons for a new altar screen, on which five icons were suspended from the architrave; the *typikon* (rule) of the monastery of Bachkovo (Bulgaria, 1081) laid down that candles were to be lit at a certain time before the icons of St George and the Crucifixion on the altar screen (*en tois kankellois...*); the church of St George inside the fortress of the little town of Yeraki (12th–13th c.) has preserved icons painted on plaster panels (the Virgin Glykophilonsa, Christ Pantocrator) placed between the marble columns of the altar screen, while its lateral columns are painted with fresco-icons of warrior saints. Icons that were painted on wood and attached to the altar screen for

centuries retained their original subject matter and arrangement in the lower areas, but also extended them into higher zones. The paintings on the screen were surmounted by the cross, the symbol of Christ's sacrifice for the redemption of mankind, the sign with which all prayers began and ended. The painted cross, preserved at Sinai from the late 12th century, testifies to the former extensive representation of Christ's Passion, on the top of the altar screen. This is still frequently found in Italian painted altar crosses in the 13th century, but in Orthodox churches in the Balkans, Christ's Passion was always reduced in later times to the basic picture of the Crucifixion. The famous carved and painted crosses preserved in the Holy Mountain and Balkan churches of the 15th to 17th centuries emphasize the figures of Christ, the Virgin and St John the Evangelist, or the crucified figure of Christ and symbolic images of the evangelists, focusing on the essence of the event, the representation of the sacrifice, which is also stressed in the liturgical rites.

The icons, cross, royal doors (usually painted with the Annunciation, and in later periods with other subjects as well) and the hangings were all parts of the altar screen which concealed the secret part of the liturgy, in accordance with the form of worship laid down in Constantinople. It was Greek bishops who brought literacy, church services, books and icons to the converted Bulgars (863), the Russians in Kiev (988) and other Slavs in the Balkans. The powerful influence radiating from the Church of Constantinople in the 11th and 12th centuries opened up new routes for works of art to the distant Romance, Slav and Georgian regions. From the Byzantine capital the highly-prized "metropolitan icons" reached Italy, Kiev, Suzdal and Novgorod in the north, Ohrid in the south, Kherson and Georgia in the east, together with instructions on the position they should occupy on the altar screen or on special stands in front of it. Thanks to the strong influence exerted by the Constantinople Church in the 11th century, the same customs regarding the decoration of the altar screen were observed in Georgia, Russia, the Balkans and Italy. This uniformity later disappeared: in the East the altar screen increased in height and the altar was concealed from view by icons and hangings, while in the West, icons were transferred to the altar itself and the screen became lower and unadorned, revealing the rites of the liturgy.

In Italy, where the liturgy and use of icons gradually underwent changes following the Schism of 1054, the impact of Constantinopolitan painting continued to be felt until the end of the 13th century. The 13th-century Italian Madonnas of Lucca and Florence, as well as those from southern Italy, are still closely dependent on Byzantine models. Artists in the workshop of the Berlinghieri family (where the famous Madonna now in the Straus collection in New York originated) and the "Bigalo Master" in Florence clearly followed experienced Byzantine painters, though some distinctive Romanesque qualities are also evident in their work. A love of ornamentation, the arabesque, and the play of line distinguishes the Italian painters of the Madonna from their Byzantine counterparts. Whereas Italian artists endeavoured, by means of the posture and gaze of the Madonna, to establish a relationship with the observer, the Byzantine master deliberately avoided any such contact, stressing the total preoccupation of the figures with another world. While, for instance, the Byzantine painter of the Virgin with Christ and angels (mid-12th c. icon, Sinai) used a mass of tiny gold lines to give radiance to his figures and merge them into the glittering light of the gold background, thereby enhancing the impression of the immaterial and unreal, Coppo di Marcovaldo used gold hatching to highlight the bodily contours of the painted figures, deliberately heightening their three-dimensional appearance, and at the same time using the gold to ornamental effect.

The extent of Byzantine influence in the 13th century on the painting of the Crusaders, who ruled Constantinople from 1204 to 1261, on the art of the Franks who occupied Greece, and on painting in Italy is illustrated by the icons with scenes from the lives of saints.

Originating in antiquity and fostered in Byzantium and many Christian regions in the Middle Ages, such paintings depicted a saint in the central field framed by tiny scenes of episodes from his or her life. Under Byzantine influence, in various periods this type of icon was popular in the Balkans, in Italy, on Cyprus, in Russia, Georgia and elsewhere. Icons of patron saints, particularly St Nicholas, the guardian of sailors, St George, the protector of farmers, and the Virgin Mary were painted in this fashion in the Balkans and Russia as late as the 18th century. In the same manner as pagan artists had depicted the figures and acts of Dionysius, Hercules and other heroes of antiquity, so Christians represented their saints in the Middle Ages. When Serbian artists began painting the life and miracles of St Sava, the first Serbian archbishop, and of his father, St Simeon (Stefan Nemanja), the first Serbian saint and founder of the royal Nemanjić dynasty, they adopted the same type of composition. One such icon, from 1645, is preserved in Morača monastery (Montenegro). In Russia, where specially revered Greek saints had been painted in this manner from early times, the format was used for icons celebrating the cult of local saints: Boris and Gleb (14th-c. icon, Tretyakov Gallery), Metropolitan Alexius of Moscow (late 15th-c. icon, Tretyakov Gallery) and others. In Italy there are similar icons honouring St Francis of Assisi (icon, Assisi, c. 1270 and Pisa, c. 1260–1270), St Catherine (Pisan icon, mid-13th c.) and other saints. In Byzantine painting and in the art of other peoples influenced by it, many compositions and forms testify, like this icon, to the adoption of the classical heritage and enduring respect for traditions.

Constantinople played an exceptional role as guardian of the cultural heritage. The imperial library, painting workshops, and the works of architecture and art in the city, which provided innumerable generations of artists and craftsmen with their knowledge, skill and inspiration, formed an inestimable treasure-house from which they drew according to their needs and the requirements of a particular age. In this great heritage, the painters of Constantinople could always find forms to satisfy the artistic concepts of a particular period. One of these, however, remained unchanged in Byzantine painting – the aspiration towards the abstract ideal, the prototype. Using the human figure to illuminate the prototype, the artists with great ingenuity and by various devices eliminated or toned down the realistic impression of space, and endowed their attenuated, weightless figures with a pronounced spirituality, enhanced by the radiance of gold or the reflection of bright vermilion or pale ochre backgrounds. The harmony of the abstract ideal and dematerialized human figure conveying a religious message was achieved most successfully at the end of the 11th century in works created in the Byzantine capital.

Many icons must have been painted in the 11th century, not only for the restored and new churches and monasteries in the capital, but also for the many new episcopal sees through which the patriarchate of Constantinople extended its influence, especially amongst the Slavs and Bulgars. One icon from this period dedicated to the Forty Martyrs is preserved in Ohrid (Macedonia). This subject, rare in icons, is also illustrated in the frescoes of the north chapel of St Sophia's in Ohrid, which are also from the 11th century, indicating that the cult of these soldier-martyrs was very popular in the Ohrid archbishopric. The icon shows the almost naked soldiers freezing to death on the frozen Lake of Sebaste, scorning death and true to their faith. The 11th-century artist, glorifying the renunciation of all earthly things, reduces the figures to basic contours and suggests human pain and suffering only by a few conventional means – the down-curving eyebrows, the hollows under the eyes, the slightly bent heads, and certain gestures, such as the hands crossed on the chest, resting on the cheek or beard, or raised in supplication to Christ.

The human qualities ascribed to martyrs, saints, Christ and the Virgin differ considerably from period to period, but are most pronounced in the latter half of the 12th century, and again around 1300, when Constantinople exerted a powerful influence on the art of the far-flung Orthodox lands for the last time. In the age of late Comnenian and early Palaeologan art, the serene harmony of 11th-century art was replaced by efforts to achieve, by all possible means, a convincing representation of suffering and an authentic depiction of events. In the icons of this period, Christ and the witnesses of his life were given very human characteristics. In the 11th century, in contrast, these figures, endowed with an unearthly calm and serenity, had emphasized the gulf between the faithful and their ideals. In Byzantine painting, the same personages of Christian history, the same events, often depicted in an identical iconographic formula, are nevertheless imbued with a great variety of feelings. The Virgin with Christ was a subject painted innumerable times, but each gifted artist left the imprint of his own emotions and ideas, his own vision of faith and life, when representing the eternal theme in his own way. Thus, notwithstanding the stylistic features imposed by the concepts of a particular age or environment, an anonymous icon painter could distinguish himself by the power of his talent and, like all true artists, create works to which modern man can respond.

In the 11th and 12th centuries, the earliest centres of icon painting appeared in Russia. At St Sophia's and Pecher monastery in Kiev, icon production must already have been considerable in the latter half of the 11th century. The earliest, though indirect, surviving evidence of religious paintings from Pecher may be a miniature in the so-called Trier Psalter, now kept at Cividale, to which miniatures were added (c. 1078–1087) when it was in the possession of Gertrude, wife of Grand Prince Izyaslav of Vishgorod (Kiev). This miniature of the Virgin with Infant enthroned, calm and dignified in a majestic frontal pose, might have been very similar to the Pecher icon of the Virgin. The few surviving 12th-century icons from Russian workshops depict saints with the same calm, fixed expression, huge eyes and strict symmetry. The ideal of 11th-century Byzantine painting long continued to suit the taste of devout Russian patrons of art. The celebrated Virgin of the Sign known as Grand Panaghia, now in the Tretyakov Gallery, illustrates the early Russian icon painters' conception of the exalted beauty of the austere Virgin set against a gold background. The finest Russian icons of the pre-Mongol period were painted in Kiev, Vladimir, Yaroslavl and Novgorod. The basic compositions and painting techniques were taken from Byzantine masters, but the experience acquired was soon applied to the painting of icons celebrating local saints.

Ancient chronicles record that a number of icons of the Virgin were brought to Kiev from Constantinople. One of these has been preserved. It was taken from Kiev by Prince Andrei Bogolubski when he left his father for his native Vladimir, in the principality of Suzdal. Prince Andrei had this icon ornamented with gold and precious stones, silver and pearls, and, following the custom of Byzantine emperors, he made it the palladium of his state, carrying it on military campaigns and venerating it in the Greek manner. Later, in 1395, this icon was brought to Moscow on the very day that the conqueror Tamerlane withdrew with his Mongols from the capital of the Russian principality. The coincidence further enhanced the fame of this celebrated icon, named the Virgin of Vladimir, which is now kept in the Tretyakov Gallery in Moscow. Only the central section of the original icon with the figures of the Virgin and Christ has survived: the removal and replacement over the centuries of the mount and sheathing, repainting and damage have changed the other parts of this, the oldest Constantinopolitan icon preserved in Russia.

Besides Kiev, Vladimir played an extremely important role in the development of 12th-century Russian art. Prince Vsevolod of Vladimir spent his youth in the Byzantine capital, his son, Constantine, spoke excellent Greek, and the prince's brother, Michael, founded the Vladimir library with over one thousand Greek codices. The surviving icons of the Vladimir-Suzdal school are of exceptional beauty and testify to the artists' perfect understanding of the Greek idea of the icon as a reflection of the otherworldly, of the endlessly repeated similarity which ensures even later icons the veneration that is intended for the prototypes, i.e. the inhabitants of the heavenly kingdom. Serene, exalted figures, symmetrically arranged, their robes bathed in the radiance of the gold background, remained characteristic of Russian painting until the arrival of the Mongols in the mid-13th century. In this early period a number of subjects and techniques were developed which, notwithstanding all the similarities with Constantinople, set Russian icon painters apart. This is most clearly seen in the local subjects, such as SS Boris and Gleb, canonized by the Russian Church as early as 1071. The cult of these two sons of Grand Prince Vladimir of Kiev, murdered on the orders of their brother, Sviatopolk, quickly spread. Their icons were painted throughout the 12th century, and in 1200 Archbishop Anthony of Novgorod journeyed to Constantinople to pray before one of their icons kept in St Sophia's. This pilgrim and travel chronicler from distant Novgorod recorded that in this church worshippers could purchase icons of Boris and Gleb made for that purpose. Their unusual clothing – caftan, cloak, fur cap and red boots – distinguished them from all the familiar Greek saints and helped to make them well known. Numerous later icons, repeating the original form, testify to the wide popularity of the Kiev saints, who were also depicted in frescoes in the Serbian monastery of Mileševa in the 1220s.

Latin rule in Constantinople and Mongol rule in Russia precluded close cultural ties between them around the middle of the 13th century, and after 1261, when a new wave of Byzantine painting appeared, Russia seems to have been tardy in adopting its innovations. Not until 1338 is there any mention of Greek artists in Russia: Isaiah in Novgorod and a group of painters working for Metropolitan Theognostes in Moscow. Slow to gain acceptance in Russia, the new style of the Palaeologan Renaissance in icons, frescoes and miniatures introduced lively, well-rounded, dynamic figures set in a clearly defined space, and a large number of participants in scenes, in order to illustrate events as fully and convincingly as possible. Icon painters used light, colour, line and perspective (orthogonal and reversed simultaneously) to achieve "authenticity" and a convincing presentation of the events of Christian history. This style spread far and wide from Constantinople, and was adopted by all artists and painters in the eastern Christian lands that maintained contacts with the city towards the end of the 13th century.

On Serbian territory, where artistic activity had been flourishing since the late 12th century, thanks to the patronage of local rulers and dignitaries, the new style penetrated rapidly. Surviving icons from the late 13th and early 14th centuries bear witness to the close similarity in the conception and composition of icons in Constantinople, Salonica and Ohrid, or at the court of King Milutin of Serbia around 1300. The Ohrid icons of the Virgin Peribleptos, the Apostle Matthew and others are masterpieces that were venerated and admired by the local people and many pilgrims. A large number of icons painted in the town or brought there from Constantinople or from Thessaloniki have been preserved in Ohrid down to the present day. It was undoubtedly an extremely important Byzantine centre of artistic activity in the late 13th and first half of the 14th centuries. The archbishops and local feudal lords endowed the Ohrid churches with many icons by the finest painters of the age. Some stood on altar screens or were placed in special frames called iconostases in the 14th century (later the term "iconostasis" was used for the altar screen itself), while others were suspended from circular candelabra or displayed on stands (Greek, *analogion*). Patriarch Makarios of Antioch travelled to Russia in the mid-17th century with his son, Archdeacon Paul of Aleppo, who left an interesting account of their journey. In St Sophia's in Novgorod, in the churches of the Holy Archangels and the Annunciation in Moscow, and in many others, the travellers saw silver and gilt boxes, similar to books, covered with velvet and brocade. Each contained twelve icons (or six if painted on both sides) depicting all the saints and feasts celebrated throughout the year. Each month the sexton would take from a box the appropriate icon and place it on an analogion, displaying the correct side if it was a bilateral icon. A candle would always burn in front of it. "There are such boxes in every church, and not just one but three or four, differing in appearance and size. They are kept on the shelves of the analogion under special cloths, in front of the altar doors." We may assume that this custom existed in Russia long before the 17th century, when Paul of Aleppo recorded it, and in other countries as well. Many still insufficiently studied icons which are considered unlikely to have found a place on the altar screen can be explained as feast-day icons that were displayed on such stands. Since the entire church calendar is painted on them, they are also a valuable source of information on certain cults that were not universal.

Only very famous miracle-working icons have a topographic element in their names, such as the Virgins of Vladimir, the Don, Tolga and Belozersk in Russia, the Pelagonitissa in Macedonia, the Studenica and Chilandar Virgins in Serbia, the Hagiosoritissa, Blacherniotissa and others in Constantinople. In other Christian lands, too, miracle-working icons were named in this way in all ages. However, in the period of Palaeologan art, it became customary to apply other epithets to icons of Christ and the Virgin, emphasizing their similarity to common humanity in their capacity to feel. The Virgin, in particular, was often given such epithets originating from Byzantine hymnography: the Swift Helper, the Indicator of the Way Full of Grace, Source of Life, Saviour of Souls, the Virgin of Tenderness, the Virgin Suckling, the All-seeing, Virgin of Intercession, All Worthy of Praise, etc. By their adoption of the cults of certain saints and by giving Christ and the Virgin certain special epithets, the various national Churches and individual donors introduced into the existing Christian iconography certain features typical of a particular society. In the later Middle Ages, works of art were commissioned by an ever wider circle of patrons – not only rulers, but also feudal landowners, nobles and bishops. In the 13th, 14th and 15th centuries, icons from the Balkans much more frequently bear the artist's signature. The emergence of artists from long centuries of anonymity was a consequence of the changed view of their role in society, regardless of whether they were monks or laymen. At Ohrid and in Moriovo in Macedonia, the painter John (Ioannis) signed his icons in 1266–1267, as did Metropolitan Jonh (Iovan) and his brother Makarios (Makarije) at the end of the 14th and beginning of the 15th centuries. In Russia, there are many records of artists, the most famous being Theophanes the Greek, who came from Constantinople at the end of the 14th century and worked in Novgorod and also in Moscow, where many patrons encouraged the flourishing artistic activity of that period. Though Theophanes signed few of his works, our knowledge of this outstanding painter is augmented by written sources. Together with local masters he painted icons, many frescoes and miniatures for Russian patrons. After Theophanes came the most famous Russian icon painter, Andrei Rublev, a monk in Holy Trinity monastery founded by Sergei of Radonezh. Unlike the works in the Constantinopolitan tradition from monastic workshops, such as those of the altar screen of Visotski monastery, or those of Theophanes the Greek, Rublev's painting is distinguished by emotional sensitivity, soft modelling, purity of line, and radiant patches of colour. These harmonious, light, lyrical colours were to remain characteristic of Russian painting throughout the 15th century. Rublev worked together with his fellow monk, Danil, with whom he had shared the experience of ascetic exploits. Rublev's fame spread in the 16th century, when he was cited as a model to be emulated by later generations of painters. The synod of 1551 even laid down that "artists should paint icons in accordance with the old traditions followed by the Greek masters and Andrei Rublev".

The century of outstanding icon painting among the Russians ends with Dionisi, active during the flourishing of the Moscow principality in the reign of Ivan III (1462–1505), when many other Russian principalities were annexed to it. After the fall of Constantinople and the Byzantine Empire in 1453, Moscow laid claim to be the "Third Rome" and the leading country of Orthodoxy, the heir of the Byzantine Empire. In 1492 Metropolitan Zosimm referred to Ivan III as "Lord and Ruler of all Russia" and "the new Emperor Constantine", and to Moscow as "the new city of Constantine". The origin of the Muscovite princes was traced back to the Roman emperor, Augustus, thereby justifying their claim to the title of emperor (tsar). At this time Moscow was a vast workshop: many churches were adorned with icons, and the painter Dionisi was employed by the court as the finest artist of his age, who sincerely respected the ancient canons, glorifying the prototypes of his icons by representing them as majestic, dematerialized figures painted in soft, light, lyrical hues.

The echoes of the Italian Renaissance did not become clearly perceptible until c. 1500, in the icons of the Italo-Byzantine school on Cyprus, ruled by Frankish kings from 1192 to 1489, and then by Venice until 1571, when it was conquered by the Turks. The final phase of Constantinopolitan art, which had a strong impact on Cyprus, as well as on

Salonica, Serbia and Russia at the end of the 14th century, survived as the essence of the style which in later centuries formed the basis of Orthodox icon painting. From the middle of the 15th century, Serbia, Mistra, Moldavia, the Holy Mountain and Russia, in their isolated artistic milieux, developed distinctive features in their icon painting while continuing to respect the fundamental ideas and iconography derived from Constantin ople. With the Turkish conquest of the Balkans and fall of Serbia in 1459, the circle of wealthy art patrons vanished, and with them the great artists. The main centres of icon painting were now in Russia, Venice and Moldavia, on Crete and Cyprus, and periodically on Mount Athos. During the 16th century, icons were painted in all Orthodox lands, but their quality depended on the level of sophistication of the patrons and artists, who in many regions of the Orthodox world were far away from the advanced thinkers and artists of Italy. Faithful to the centuries-old ideals of the Neo-Platonists and Byzantine theologians, the 16th-and 17th-century painters in eastern Europe and on the Greek islands only partially accepted a few features of the Renaissance and Baroque styles. To satisfy the taste of Mediterranean patrons, the 16th-century Italo-Greek painters on Cyprus introduced many contemporary features in the minor decorative parts of the icon or in the dress of the donor, shown kneeling before his patron saint. In the works of the famous Greek Venetian masters gathered at the Greek monastery of St George, a compromise between Byzantine and 17th-century European painting undermined the ideal of the Byzantine icon. Attempts to present landscape, a realistic relationship of man and nature, and the use of perspective destroyed the fundamental concept of the holy image. The works of the well-known Italo-Greek masters of the 17th century – Theodore Poulakis, Emmanuel Zanfurnaris, Emmanuel Tzanes Victor of Crete, Elijah Moscos, Jeremias Palladas, Apakas, Lombardos, Emmanuel Tzanes and others – like those of their predecessors, Andreas (c. 1421–1492) and Nicholas Ritzos, are simply a series of unhappy attempts to combine two worlds whose aesthetic standpoints and ideas were incompatible. These new artistic conceptions reached the monks of the Holy Mountain, where the so-called Italo-Cretan or Italo-Greek painters were often employed in the 16th and 17th centuries, and made their appearance in Russia in the 17th century, provoking a conflict of the old and new ideas. From the account of Paul of Aleppo we can see the extent to which these ideological and aesthetic contradictions agitated the clergy and painters in Moscow. In 1654 Patriarch Nikon, incensed by these new trends in painting, ordered all such icons "which some Muscovite icon painters have begun to paint, copying Frankish and Polish pictures" to be forcibly removed from private homes and churches, the eyes of saints painted in this manner to be gouged out, and the icons carried through the city with loud warnings as to the penalty that awaited any icon painter who failed to respect the old style. Patriarch Nikon even preached a sermon before the tsar on the illegality of the new painting resembling western works. He hurled these discredited icons on a metal plaque on the floor, broke them and ordered them to be burnt.

The conflict of the old and new in the 17th century was more keenly felt in Russia than elsewhere, dividing people into opposing camps, causing quarrels, and inspiring a great many theological texts on the concept of the image, the origin of art in general, and the purpose of artistic activity. The treatises of Simon Ushakov, Simeon of Polotsk, the protopresbyter Avakum, Karion Istomin and Tsar Alexis Mikhailovich himself testify to the enormous importance ascribed to the concept of the icon. Once again the ideology of the church establishment, supported by the tsar, won the day, reaffirming that "the first artist is God himself: wishing to create man, he created him in his own image and form. And thus the prototype of man is God himself... For this reason, the icon or picture is an imitation or copy. This is how the icon (which in Greek means both image and resemblance) got its name." Simon Ushakov also declared that "God gave man the spiritual power called imagination to draw the forms of various things: he endowed individuals, though not all in equal measure, with the natural gift of creating figures and, by means of various forms of art, of making the imaginary world visible."

In the 17th century there were still icon painters who by the strength of their convictions and talent attained the level of the Byzantine Orthodox artists. Later the educated classes no longer understood the meaning of the Byzantine forms, but these survived in folk art into the 19th century.

MAJOR ICON COLLECTIONS

Created for the needs of the Church or devout patrons who wished to have an icon in their homes, many of these Christian cult paintings did not remain in their original circle. The devastations of war, plundering, the destruction of churches and homes periodically afflicted all regions over the centuries. Icons were carried off as spoils or were sent to other places or countries as gifts, making it difficult today to ascertain the origin even of those preserved on church iconostases or in monastery treasuries. Since the end of the 19th century, many have found a place in museums as valuable works of art.

Large icon collections have been preserved down to the present time in the monasteries of Mount Athos, at St Catherine's on Sinai, in the Meteora monasteries in Greece, the monastery of St John the Theologian on Patmos, in churches and monasteries on Cyprus, and in many monasteries in Greece, the Balkans, in Russia and as far away as Georgia in the Caucasus. In these ancient centres of the Eastern Orthodox faith, icons have been preserved in their original places, but equally valuable and interesting icon collections can be seen in contemporary museums, where increasing attention is paid to the study and display of these medieval works of art.

The huge and exceptionally valuable collection of icons in the monastery of St Catherine on Sinai became more widely known among art lovers and scholars only in the 1950s, when the Greek archaeologists Georgios and Maria Sotiriou published their book on the Sinai icons. Following the cleaning of these icons from centuries of sooty deposits left by candle-smoke and the removal of poor restoration work carried out in earlier times, which was undertaken between 1958 and 1965 by experts from the Universities of Alexandria, Michigan and Princeton, about 2000 icons from the 6th to the 18th centuries were revealed in their original state. The protection and study of these art treasures have been continued since then by the Greek Archaeological Service in Athens. The greatest attention of experts has focused on the oldest Sinai icons in encaustic (melted-wax) technique, which are extremely rare. Icons were brought to St Catherine's, founded by Emperor Justinian I (527–565), from all parts of the Christian East, and some were painted in the monastery itself. The death of Father Pachomius, the last surviving icon painter at Sinai, in 1960, brought to an end the centuries-old tradition of Byzantine icon painting in this ancient monastery.

The monasteries of Mount Athos have retained their traditional way of life, rites and most of their architecture and works of art, including icons, but because of difficulty of access their icon collections have not been fully studied. The ancient monastery of St John the Theologian on Patmos is mentioned in the early 13th century as having a large number of icons, but today it has only four from the earlier period (11th–13th c.), in addition to a large number from the post-Byzantine era (15th–18th c.). The latter, over 150, include the works of famous Italo-Cretan painters: Andreas Ritzos (15th c.), Nicholas Ritzos (late 15th c.), Nicholas Tzafouris (late 15th c.), Michael Damaskinos (second half of the 16th c.), George Klotzas (second half of the 16th c.), Thomas Vathas (second half of the 16th c.), John Apakas (early 17th c.), Jeremias Palladas (early 17th c.), Emmanuel Tzanes (second half of the 17th c.), Theodore Poulakis (second half of the 17th c.) and others. The icons of this monastery have been studied and published, unlike the many exceptional works on the Holy Mountain, where conservation and investigation work is still underway. The few partial studies published indicate the value of the vast art treasures of Athos.

Numerous icons from the 9th to 17th centuries have been preserved in the churches and monasteries on Cyprus. The finest and most famous of these are undoubtedly those on the original iconostasis of the little cave church of the hermitage of St Neophytos at Paphos, from 1183, but many other notable works are to be found in the churches of the Greek Orthodox population in Azinou, Nicosia, Lefkonia, Lagudera, in the villages of Pendula, Pelendri, Moutoula, Kakopetria, Kalopanayotis and elsewhere.

Among the museum collections in Greece, the most important, in view of the number and antiquity of its icons, is in the Byzantine Museum in Athens, founded in 1920, when the treasures of medieval art gathered from the end of the 19th century by the Christian Archaeological Society and small museums throughout the country were brought together in one place. Under a law passed in 1920, the Byzantine Museum in Athens was made responsible for preserving and exhibiting objects of Byzantine culture found in Greece. Since then, the icon collection has been considerably enriched by bequests and now displays the works of icon painters of the Byzantine and post-Byzantine periods, from the 9th to the 18th centuries. In addition to icons by anonymous, often outstanding, artists of the earlier period (9th–15th c.) the collection contains works by the famous Italo-Cretan masters Michael Damaskinos (second half of the 16th c.), Emmanuel Lambardos (late 16th–early 17th c.), Emmanuel Tzanes (second half of the 17th c.), Victor of Crete (17th c.), and other artists of the Cretan school who have remained anonymous.

Another major collection in Athens is housed in the Benaki Museum, named after its founder and owner. This contains a large number of icons, particularly of the post-Byzantine period, signed by 16th- and 17th-century artists: the hieromonk Philip, George Kortez, Emmanuel Lambardos, Peter Lambardos, Emmanuel Zanfurnaris, Elijah Moskos, Leo Moskos, Emmanuel Tzanes, Master Victor of Crete, Luke Mavrikis, the hieromonk Pigasios, Theodore Poulakis, John Moscos, Stephen Tzankarolas and others. The masters of the Cretan school, exceptionally well represented in this Athenian collection, were often members of the same family, whose talents and skill were passed down from father to son.

The Soviet Union has many large and very important collections of Russian, Byzantine and other icons. Museums in all the major cities have icon collections, some of which are of exceptional value. One such is in the Hermitage, one of the world's great museums, housed in the former imperial palace in Leningrad, which was open to visitors as early as 1852. The famous icons in this museum are from collections formed in the 18th century. The small Byzantine cameo and stone icons in the Hermitage, for example, were part of the personal collection of Empress Catherine II, while the Byzantine mosaic icons, enamels and other precious objects belonged to the private collection of the famous art connoisseur, A.P. Bazilevski, which came into the possession of the Hermitage in 1885. At the beginning of the 20th century, it acquired the celebrated Byzantine icons from the collection of the eminent Byzantologist, N.P. Likhachov, and in 1931 the collections of the Russian Archaeological Institute in Istanbul were transferred there. Through the reorganization of the state museums in 1930 and 1934, the Hermitage acquired major collections of Byzantine and post-Byzantine icons previously kept in the Russian State Museum. These additions over the years have made the Hermitage one of the world's leading museums in which icons are studied and exhibited. The Russian Museum in Leningrad had begun collecting Russian works of art, primarily icons, as early as 1898, and was particularly enriched by the gift of N.P. Likhachov's collection of Russian icons in 1913. Today this collection numbers over seven thousand. Huge icon collections are also found in the museums of Moscow. In 1924 the History Museum opened a Byzantine art gallery exhibiting works that had been privately owned before the Revolution. This museum now has around thirteen thousand Russian, Byzantine and other icons from various periods. The churches and museums of the Kremlin likewise house several thousand icons, including some outstanding 12th-century Byzantine examples. The Andrei Rublev Museum, also in Moscow, contains a notable collection of Russian icons, while the A.S. Pushkin State Art Museum includes some icons brought from the Holy Mountain in the 1850s by the eminent scholar, P.I. Sevastyanov. Immediately after the Revolution, the famous Tretyakov Gallery in Moscow was entrusted with the safe-keeping of the finest Russian icons from churches and monasteries that fell into disuse. It thus acquired icons from Visotski, Holy Trinity-Sergiev and other monasteries, among them the most famous holy picture in all Russia, the Virgin of Vladimir, painted in Constantinople in the late 11th century. The several thousand icons in this collection have long attracted the attention of scholars and art lovers.

The former monastery originally dedicated to the Holy Trinity and then to its founder, Sergei of Radonezh, now houses an exhibition of Byzantine and Russian icons, as part of the Zagorsk State Museum. In the 1930s over a hundred old icons from this monastery were transferred to state museums or disappeared, but despite this loss the collection is one of exceptional importance. It originated in the late Middle Ages when it was customary for Russian princely families to donate icons to the monastery where their members were buried: the personal icon of the deceased was taken with the body to the monastery and remained there. Icon painters are known to have lived and worked in this monastery in the 15th century, whereas in the 14th century icons were brought there from various other places. The collection now numbers about 375 works from the 14th to 17th centuries, besides many of later date. Formerly all these icons were attached to the iconostases of the monastery's churches or hung on the walls, especially in the cathedral church of the Holy Trinity and the church of the Assumption, but also in the monastery chapels. This Russian monastery founded in the 14th century has preserved such famous works as the Holy Trinity icon by Andrei Rublev, the Virgin of the Don, the Virgin of Tikhvin and others. Between 1425 and 1427 Andrei Rublev and Danil Tchorni painted icons for the monastery, forty-two of which are to be found today. The most important of these still stand on the early 15th-century iconostasis in Holy Trinity church. The number of valuable works preserved here and its religious and artistic traditions make the Holy Trinity-Sergiev monastery a monument of exceptional distinction.

When visiting holy places, travellers, art lovers and collectors in the 19th century showed a great interest in icons. One of these was the famous self-taught art connoisseur and collector who travelled widely in Orthodox lands, Archimandrite, later Bishop, Porfiri Uspenski. From the Sinai monastery of St Catherine he procured several encaustic icons which after the Revolution were placed in the Museum of Western and Eastern Art in Kiev, where they are kept today. These sixth/seventh-century works in this ancient Mediterranean technique have attracted much attention from scholars and art experts.

The Novgorod History and Architecture Museum, housed in Novgorod Fortress, inherited art treasures gathered in the 19th century. The major part of the Museum of Antiquities, founded in Novgorod as early as 1865, comprised collections of icons. The first icon exhibition to be organized was held in this city in 1911. The museum's inventory listed four hundred icons in 1916, and by the eve of the Second World War, three thousand. During the war, it lost the greater part of its exhibits, and now has only a few outstanding icons from the 12th, 13th and later centuries. In other cities of the old Russian principalities many museums preserve notable collections of icons, mostly on wood. In Georgia, however, in Tbilisi, Kutaisi and the churches of Upper Svanetia, there are thousands of Georgian and Byzantine icons sheathed in silver and gilded, with sections in enamel, testifying to the outstanding craftsmanship of ancient Georgia, where metal-working flourished alongside painting in the Middle Ages.

The great museums of western Europe, established in countries where the phenomenon of the icon had a much briefer tradition than in the East, do not possess large icon collections, but contain a number of works of exceptional value. The Louvre in Paris has some sixth/seventh-century Coptic icons, an unusual circular icon (tondo) of St George from the 14th century, some small ivory icons and other Byzantine and Russian works, while the Victoria and Albert Museum in London houses an extremely valuable collection of Byzantine cameos and small icons from the 9th to 12th centuries, 14th-century icons on wood, etc. Valuable Byzantine mosaic icons are kept in the museum of Florence cathedral, in the State Museum in Berlin (which also has Byzantine ivory icons), and in various private collections. The Vatican Museum has some exceptionally fine examples, and an encaustic icon from the sixth/seventh century is to be found in the church of S. Maria Nuova in Rome. Because of its commercial and political interests, Venice over a long period maintained the closest contacts with Constantinople and with the Greek islands, where the art of icon painting survived into the 17th and early 18th centuries. In consequence, the Venetian collections, especially in the treasury of S. Marco and in the Greek monastery of St George, have preserved a considerable number of icons of the Byzantine and post-Byzantine periods. The most famous is the *pala d'oro*, a gold iconostasis of quite small size with numerous holy figures, brought from Constantinople after the Latin conquest in the 13th century, which is now in the treasury of S. Marco. This also contains other precious Byzantine works, among them icons of mosaic and tempera on wood with costly silver and gilt sheathing. The National Museum in Ravenna, the Museo di Palazzo Venezia in Rome, the Archaeological Museum and Museo Civico Correr in Venice, the Museo del Bargello in Milan, Museo Provinciale in Torcello, the Museum of the Hellenistic Institute for Byzantine and Post-Byzantine Studies in Venice and many churches in Italy contain notable works of icon painting in the metropolitan or Italo-Byzantine style, as well as some portable mosaic icons from Constantinople.

Collections of Byzantine icons are also kept in the renowned Art History Museum (Kunsthistorisches Museum) in Vienna and in museums in Stockholm, Oslo, Bergen, Dublin, Munich (Bayerisches Nationalmuseum and Stadtmuseum), Recklinghausen (Ikonenmuseum), Freising, Geneva, and other European cities.

Yugoslavia has a large number of Byzantine and Serbian icons from the 9th to early 18th centuries. The finest examples originating in Constantinople are displayed in the gallery near the church of the Virgin Peribleptos (now St Clement's) in Ohrid (Macedonia), in which icons of the Palaeologan period predominate, in the National Museum in Belgrade, the Museum of Macedonia in Skopje, the Museum of the Serbian Orthodox Church in Belgrade, the Orthodox Church Museum in Dubrovnik, in Sarajevo and in collections in Zadar. In Bulgaria, in addition to icons in churches and monasteries, there are major icon exhibitions in the Alexander Nevski church and the Church Museum in Sofia. In Romania, many icons are displayed in monastery treasuries and municipal museums, the most important in this respect being the National Museum in Bucharest.

Not attempting to list all the notable public and private collections, we have simply mentioned the most important ones in Europe. We shall not describe the collections in the United States of America, the most interesting of which is at Dumbarton Oaks in Washington, or those in Tokyo (National Museum of Western Arts), in Melbourne, or some other cities around the world since, apart from the Dumbarton Oaks Centre for Byzantine Studies, they publish only periodic information on their wealth. The Orthodox diaspora has led to icons being taken to distant countries that differ in their spiritual heritage and historical traditions from the Mediterranean world in which the icon originated. But in the world of today, with its intermingling of languages, cultures and traditions, the travels of the icon to all parts of the globe testify to the cultural and artistic value it holds for our contemporaries.

Much more about the art of the icon remains to be discovered and explained by scholars and art experts. When the collections of the Holy Mountain monasteries become more accessible and their vast art treasures are fully studied, another important step will be taken towards understanding the beauty of that long-vanished world.

1 The Forty Martyrs of Sebaste

Tempera on wood. 44 × 33.5 cm. 11th c. Ohrid, Icon Gallery, Yugoslavia. Legends in Greek.

The icon was probably painted for the Ohrid cathedral of St Sophia, where the Forty Martyrs of Sebaste were particularly venerated. A complete cycle of frescoes illustrating the fate of these soldiers who, with one exception, chose to freeze to death on the lake of Sebaste rather than renounce their faith, was painted in the north-eastern chapel (at ground level beside the altar) of St Sophia's in the 11th century. The crowning with the victor's wreath with which Christ rewards martyrs is a symbolic scene expressing the essential idea of this hagiographic cycle. In the fresco cycle in the chapel, it occupied the semi-dome of the apse, while in icons it appears as an independent symbolic entity. The proposed dating of the icon is based on stylistic features, the modelling of the naked bodies, the manner of expressing suffering by gestures, and the typical faces with huge eyes.

2 The Archangel Gabriel from the Annunciation

Tempera on wood with revêtement. 111.5 × 67.5 cm. Early 12th c. Ohrid, Icon Gallery, Yugoslavia. Legends in Greek.

With the icon of the Virgin (3), it made up the Annunciation composition which once adorned the altar screen of the Ohrid church of the Virgin Peribleptos. The 12th-c. revêtement consists of silver repoussé plaques with vegetable patterns and figures connected with the archangel: in the central field at the top there was a representation (now missing) of the Prepared Throne, while the lateral borders are decorated with figures of angels. Because of the pronounced monumentality of the figure shown in movement and the deep folds of the robes, on the one hand, and the extremely delicate modelling of the faces on the other, scholars have proposed widely differing dates for this icon — the late 11th, 12th and 13th centuries.

3 The Virgin from the Annunciation

Tempera on wood with revêtement. 111.5 × 68 cm. Early 12th c. Ohrid, Icon Gallery, Yugoslavia. Legends and donor's inscription in Greek.

With the icon of the Archangel Gabriel (2), it made up the Annunciation composition which once adorned the altar screen of the Ohrid church of the Virgin Peribleptos. The background and borders are covered with silver repoussé plaques (12th c.) with vegetable ("Blütenblatt") patterns, figures and the legend: "The Lord is with thee" (Luke I, 28). The upper border has repoussé medallions of Christ, the Virgin and St John (the Deesis) and of the Virgin's parents, Joachim and Anne. The lower border has the figures of St Andrew and St Basil, while the lateral margins contain figures of the prophets who foretold the coming of the Virgin in their writings. This subject (known since Comnenian times) was intended to point out the correspondence of the Old and New Testaments. The ornamental metal halo and the jewels on the Virgin's breast were later additions. The donor's inscription on the vertical enamel plaques reads: "Most Holy Virgin, I present to you what is yours, your faithful servant, a priest of the Lord, Leo." The poetic expression "priest of the Lord" would seem to refer to the archbishop of Ohrid who commissioned the revêtement and plaques with the inscription for this icon in the early 12th century. The delicate modelling of the flesh and pronounced folds of the drapery, on which signs of 19th-century retouching can be discerned, have led scholars to propose different dates for this icon, ranging from the late 11th to the 13th century.

4 The Raising of Lazarus

Tempera on wood. 12.5 × 24 cm. First half of the 12th c. Athens, private collection. Legends in Greek.

This small icon of one of the Twelve Feasts is considered to have once formed part of an altar screen in a church of Mount Athos. From the 11th century on, it was customary in Byzantine churches to attach icons of the major church feasts to the architrave of the altar screen. Because of its unusual vermilion background and stylistic features, scholars believe that this icon and one of the Transfiguration now in the Hermitage belonged to the same feast cycle. Its dating is based on stylistic considerations: the firmly modelled contours beneath the drapery, whose folds are emphasized by long, flowing lines, and the warm colouring and modelling of the faces with broad brush-strokes of thick paint. The facial features recall the Comnenian age, the impression of relief being achieved by new means, although without the marked linearism prevalent in the late Comnenian epoch.

5 The Virgin Hodegetria (Indicator of the Way)

Mosaic on wood. 57 × 38 cm. Late 12th c. Chilandar monastery on Mount Athos. Legends in Greek.

This icon of the Virgin Hodegetria, the patron saint of the Serbian monastery of Chilandar on Athos, is made of tesserae of coloured glass paste and tesserae in which molten gold leaf was combined with glass paste. It is assumed to have been procured for the monastery at the end of the 12th century, when the Serbian ruler Grand Prince Stefan Nemanja, having become a monk and taken the name Simeon, together with his son, the monk Sava, was supervising the completion of their foundation on the Holy Mountain. Since the main monastery church is dedicated to the Virgin Hodegetria (Indicator of the Way), the founders would have wished the patron's icon to be of costly material. The large eyes and fixed, stern expression of the Virgin in full frontal position, the precise draftsmanship of the figures and shading of the drapery, whose folds do not closely follow the contours of the body, but independently create an impression of volume, all indicate that the icon originated in some Constantinople workshop in the late 12th century.

6 St John the Baptist

Fresco. 1208–1209. Studenica monastery, church of the Mother of God, southern side of the north-western pilaster in the nave. Yugoslavia. Legends and text on the scroll in Old Serbian.

Frescoes in medieval churches often imitated the form and frame of icons when it was desired to draw special attention to a particularly revered saint. The church of the Mother of God of Studenica monastery, begun by the Grand Prince of Serbia, Stefan Nemanja, and completed by his youngest son, Sava, was painted with frescoes in 1208–1209, according to a partially preserved inscription in the drum of the dome. Several icons in fresco technique were painted beside the altar screen and on the pilasters in the western part of the nave. St John the Baptist (the Forerunner), holding a scroll with a text from the Gospel according to St Matthew (Matt. III, 2 and 10), was accorded a prominent place as the specially venerated protector of mankind, and also of the church's founders and benefactors, Nemanja and his sons, princes of the Serbian ruling family.

7 St James

Tempera on wood. 91 × 65 cm. 13th c. Monastery of St John on the island of Patmos, Greece. Legends in Greek.

The iconographic details present in this icon (Christ proffering a chalice from the heavens and blessing the apostle) indicate the ordination of James, the first archbishop of Jerusalem, a subject rarely depicted in icons. Its dating is based on stylistic analysis and comparison with frescoes at Sopoćani monastery (Serbia) and the miniatures of Psalter no. 46 in Stavronikita monastery on Mount Athos.

8 Christ Pantocrator, gift of Archbishop Constantine Cavassila

Tempera on wood. 135 × 73 cm. 1262–1263. Ohrid, Icon Gallery, Yugoslavia. Legends in Greek.

The date of this icon is recorded on the inscription on the back: "This icon was painted in the year 1262/1263 in the time of Archbishop Constantine Cavassila." It may be assumed that this eminent and most revered archbishop of Ohrid ordered the icon of Christ Pantocrator for an Ohrid church, perhaps St Sophia's. The mysterious inscription (+ X B) along the left side, painted in vermilion on the gold background, may be the artist's signature. The Greek letters O Ω N were inscribed on the Pantocrator's halo, as was customary. This is taken from Exodus III, 14, being the definition of the deity given by God to Moses on Mount Horeb. The exceptional plasticity of the form and fine modelling of the flesh, on the one hand, and the geometrical lines of the folds and gleaming patches on the robes on the other, point to a painter who followed contemporary attempts to achieve monumentality of style in the art of Constantinople, while retaining the older manner of depicting drapery.

9 St George, by the painter John

Tempera on wood. 145 × 86 cm. 1266/1267. Struga, church of St George, Yugoslavia. Legends and inscriptions in Greek.

The inscription preserved on the back of the icon records the names of the donor and artist: "The gift of your humble servant, the deacon John (Ioannes), who had the dignity of a repherendarios: when I had respectfully drawn your holy person, one skilled in the use of colours painted this icon. John lovingly addresses this prayer 1266/1267, indiktion 5. Painted by the hand of the artist John." The donor of the icon, the Ohrid deacon and repherendarios John (Ioannes), is known to have been a lover of art. He probably commissioned it in a local workshop, where the painter John was working in an old-fashioned manner, far removed from the new style that flourished in Constantinople following the renewal of the Byzantine Empire under the Palaeologue dynasty (1261).

10 St George with scenes from his Life

Tempera on wood. 109 × 72 cm. 13th c., Athens, Byzantine Museum. Legends in Greek. The icon depicts the figure, life and sufferings of St George. The figure of the saint, his halo and shield, stand out in relief from the other painted surfaces. The woman donor, shown kneeling in supplication at the saint's feet in the lower left corner, has not been identified. Her insignificance before the saint is stressed by the humility of her pose and tiny size, as well as by the absence of any inscription with her name. Although the work was found at Kastoria, the western features of the saint's military attire and the Kufic ornamentation on his shield incline experts to the view that it was painted in Jerusalem, on Cyprus or in a 13th-century Balkan workshop under Latin influence. While the treatment of the figure has marked Romanesque qualities, the iconography of the twelve scenes of the saint's life is in the Byzantine tradition.

11 Madonna with Christ

Tempera on wood. 89 × 59 cm. c. 1270–1280. Hvar, cathedral, altar of the Hektorović family. Yugoslavia.
This icon is generally considered to have originated in a Pisan workshop where Byzantine (Comnenian) conceptions of painting still prevailed in the 13th century. The bright colours and sharp contrasts, the physiognomies of the Virgin and Child, and the treatment of drapery nevertheless indicate a master working in a different environment, in which expressiveness was more important than the canons of beauty founded on the classical tradition that were respected in Constantinople in the latter half of the 13th century.

12 The Crucifixion

Tempera on wood. 87 × 61.5 cm. 13th c. Athens, Byzantine Museum. Legend in Greek.
This is a bilateral processional icon: the reverse now has a Virgin with Christ from the 16th century. The obverse with the Crucifixion has also clearly been repainted. Traces of an older work, considered to date from the ninth century, are visible on the gold background with stars. On the upper layer, ascribed to the 13th century on the basis of stylistic features, the artist was most successful with the faces of Christ, the Virgin and St John, furrowed by pain and grief, with dark green shading. The harmonious proportions of the figures, their contours exceptionally clearly defined beneath the folds of drapery, and the resonant colours exemplify the finest qualities of progressive artistic trends in the latter half of the 13th century, during the Palaeologan Renaissance of Byzantine art.

13 The Virgin with Christ

Tempera on wood. A badly damaged icon with broken edges. Second half of the 13th c. Chilandar monastery on Mount Athos.
Together with a Christ Pantocrator icon, also preserved in the Serbian monastery of Chilandar, this forms a pair of main icons on the altar screen, for which new icons seem to have been painted in the second half of the 13th century. In its stylistic features – the exceptionally delicate treatment of the faces with their perfectly symmetrical lines, the almost classical serenity of expression, and gentle harmony of warm and cool tones – this icon illustrates the contemporary idea of beauty, as seen also in the majestic mosaic Deesis in the gallery of St Sophia's in Istanbul.

14 The Virgin Hodegetria (Indicator of the Way)

Tempera on wood with revêtement. 97 × 67 cm. Second half of the 13th c. Ohrid, Icon Gallery, Yugoslavia.
This processional icon with the Crucifixion on the reverse (15) was found in the church of the Virgin Peribleptos. Only the obverse, with the specially venerated icon of the Virgin with Christ known as the Hodegetria (Indicator of the Way) was sheathed with a metal revêtement. The background and frame are covered with silver plaques executed in a workshop where the subject of the icon they would adorn does not seem to have been known in advance. The plaques consequently illustrate different themes: some have busts of saints, others scenes of Christ's life – some repeated several times, while many have repoussé ornamentation or depict the Prepared Throne. On the lower edge there is a plaque with the Virgin with Christ Enthroned with the designation EPISKEPSIS ("Over-seer"). Whereas on older Byzantine icons the revêtement was treated as part of the thematic whole, here it is simply an impressive and costly cover, an adornment of the venerated figures. The beautiful symmetrical oval face, delicate ochre and green shading, the resonant purple and green of the robes, all show the high quality of the anonymous painter.

15 The Crucifixion

Tempera on wood with canvas. 97 × 67 cm. Second half of the 13th c. Ohrid, Icon Gallery, Yugoslavia. Legends in Greek.

The Crucifixion is painted on the reverse of the Virgin Hodegetria (14), a sheathed processional icon. The exceptionally fine modelling of the flesh with gentle green and olive shading, plasticity of the figures and simplicity of the drapery, falling in wide folds, the harmony of the mainly cool shades of blue, pale green and violet against the gold background, all reveal a gifted painter who followed the classicist trends in Byzantine art in the latter half of the 13th century. The grief of the Virgin and St John is conveyed not only by the conventional gestures but by the facial expressions, testifying to the classical tradition in the works of Byzantine masters of the Palaeologan Renaissance.

16 The Evangelist Matthew

Tempera on wood. 115 × 56 cm. Late 13th or early 14th c. Ohrid, Icon Gallery, Yugoslavia. Legend in Greek.
This outstanding painting of the Evangelist Matthew in movement, a powerful figure with noble, harmonious proportions, the impression of volume skilfully conveyed by the shading of the drapery, is clearly the work of a great master. In the lower right-hand corner, on the ochre background beside the saint's left leg, there is an undeciphered Greek inscription that may be the artist's signature. The icon ranks among the finest achievements of Palaeologan art.

17 The Virgin Psychosostria (Saviour of Souls)

Tempera on wood with revêtement. 94.5 × 80.3 cm. Early 14th c. Ohrid, Icon Gallery, Yugoslavia. Legends in Greek.
This is a processional icon with the Annunciation (18) on the reverse. The background is covered with silver plaques embossed with ornamentation, busts of saints and Greek legends. The figures on the revêtement are thematically connected with the icon's subject: Christ Pantocrator (on the upper border) as ruler of the universe, the prophets who foretold the Virgin's coming (on the left side, Aaron and Gideon, on the right, Ezekiel, Daniel and Habakkuk) and holy personages in upper corners (Jacob, an Old Testament patriarch, and St John Chrysostom, who appears to have been added later). This very richly ornamented icon forms a pair with an icon of Christ Saviour of Souls (19). Both, it seems, were brought to Ohrid from Constantinople for the church of St Sophia, at the request of Archbishop Gregory of Ohrid, at the beginning of the 14th century. This Ohrid prelate is known to have been given title to the Constantinopolitan monastery of the Virgin Saviour of Souls by Emperor Andronicus II Palaeologus (1282–1328). The Virgin's epithet on this Ohrid icon indicates that it may have been a copy of the patron's icon in the Constantinopolitan monastery of the same name. With their refined colour scheme and outstanding modelling of the figures, both icons bearing this epithet of the Virgin and Christ rank among the finest works of the Palaeologan Renaissance, and may thus be attributed to a metropolitan workshop in the early 14th century. Archbishop Gregory's connections with the Byzantine capital are well attested, as is his contribution to the architectural restoration of St Sophia's in Ohrid. It is therefore very likely that he was responsible for these icons being brought to Ohrid.

18 The Annunciation

Tempera on wood. 94.5 × 80.3 cm. Early 14th c. Ohrid, Icon Gallery, Yugoslavia. Legends in Greek.
The Annunciation is on the reverse of the sheathed processional icon of the Virgin Saviour of Souls (17). Stylistic features indicate that it was painted at the same time as the latter, but it was not sheathed. The outstanding qualities of the painting – the successful creation of an impression of depth by means of painted architecture, the use of darker colours in the foreground and radiant light emanating from the background, the delicate shading of the faces – make this icon of the Annunciation one of the most beautiful works of Palaeologan art of the early 14th century. It probably originated in Constantinople.

19 Christ Psychosostis (Saviour of Souls)

Tempera on wood with revêtement. 94.5 × 80.3 cm. Early 14th c. Ohrid, Icon Gallery, Yugoslavia. Legends in Greek.
A processional icon with the Crucifixion (20) on the reverse, it was probably brought to Ohrid together with the processional icon of the Virgin Saviour of Souls at the behest of Archbishop Gregory in the early 14th century. The revêtement of silver plaques, clearly made at the same time as the painting, was subsequently damaged. The background is covered with plaques embossed with vegetable and geometrical ornamentation, and the border is decorated, as was customary with icons of Christ Pantocrator, with busts of apostles: Peter, Andrew, Paul, John the Theologian, Matthew and Mark. The regular features, delicate modelling of the flesh and excellently drawn hands, together with the powerful harmony of the complementary colours of the robes, reveal the hand of an experienced artist, probably working in a Constantinopolitan workshop.

20 The Crucifixion

Tempera on wood. 96 × 70 cm. c.1300. Ohrid, Icon Gallery, Yugoslavia. Legends in Greek.
A processional icon, the reverse of the Christ Saviour of Souls (19). The painter's mastery is demonstrated by the plasticity of Christ's body, achieved by the shading of tones from grey-green to pale ochre, and the gradual transitions from dark shades on the edge of the oval heads to the highlighted contours of the chin and cheek-bones on the faces of the Virgin and St John. Their elongated figures define the foreground area, enclosed by a painted wall. This Crucifixion and the Annunciation on the reverse of the icon of the Virgin Saviour of Souls are thought to be the work of the same painter in a Constantinopolitan workshop of the early 14th century.

21 The Ascension

Tempera on wood. 39.5 × 29 cm. c.1300. Ohrid, Icon Gallery, Yugoslavia. Legends in Greek.
This icon is believed to have been painted in c.1300 for the needs of the church of the Virgin Peribleptos (decorated with frescoes in 1295), in which it is now kept. The figures are shown in dynamic movement with lively gestures; the drama of the strange event is emphasized by various painterly means, particularly by the contrasts of the complementary colours of the clothing, with the most striking contrast in the central section, where the Virgin and Christ, in purple and dark robes respectively, stand out against the gold background. The modelling of the flesh was completed with exceptionally dramatic, swift brush-strokes of very pale ochre, highlighting the faces, necks and arms, showing that the artist was capable of working with speed and assurance. It is ascribed to Michael or Eutyches, working in the mature Palaeologan style. They left their signatures on frescoes in the church of the Virgin Peribleptos, and later were the main painters employed by King Milutin of Serbia for his foundations.

22 The Crucifixion

Tempera on wood. 33.5 × 25.5 cm. c.1300. Chapel dedicated to the Annunciation on the island of Patmos, Greece. Legends in Greek.
This small icon is considered to have formed one of the cycle of Twelve Feasts on an altar screen. Its marked narrative quality, the number of details and personages which create a convincing picture of the event, the plasticity of the figures, whose bodily contours are strongly emphasized by the drapery, the lively gestures and arrangement of the figures in the relatively deep space enclosed by a wall, the swift ochre brush-strokes highlighting the faces and bodies – all point to an excellent master working in the mature Palaeologan style.

23 The Virgin with Christ

Tempera on wood. 83 × 58 cm. Early 14th c. Athens, Byzantine Museum. Legends in Greek.
The asymmetrical features and expressive face of this Virgin do not follow the classical canon of beauty emulated in Byzantine court workshops at the end of the 13th and beginning of the 14th centuries. Such characteristics appeared in the early 14th century in the painting workshops of Salonica, where this icon seems to have originated. The dating is based on analysis of the forms and colours, the almost hard shadows around the eyes, the oval faces of the Virgin and Christ (intensifying the impression of plasticity), and the firm contours of the bodies beneath the drapery.

24 The Virgin with Christ, called EPISKEPSIS ("Over-seer")

Mosaic on wood. 95 × 62 cm. Early 14th c. Athens, Byzantine Museum. Legends in Greek.
This icon, brought to Athens from Triglia in Bythinia (Asia Minor), is made of relatively large tesserae of coloured paste and paste with gold. It is dated on the basis of the stylistic features. The epithet EPISKEPSIS ("Over-seer") does not signify a separate iconographic type of the Virgin with Christ but refers to the characteristic ascribed to her, to protect and aid those who pray to her. In the 14th century, icons of the Virgin were increasingly given epithets previously used in Byzantine rhetoric and liturgical poetry.

25 The Virgin with Christ, called EPISKEPSIS ("Over-seer")

Tempera on wood. Whole icon: 103.5 × 52.5 cm. Mid-14th c. Ohrid, Icon Gallery, Yugoslavia. Legends in Greek.
This icon from the church of the Holy Physicians (Mali Sveti Vrači) in Ohrid was transferred after cleaning to the Icon Gallery. The Virgin is shown full-length, standing and holding Christ in her right arm. The Archangels Michael and Gabriel in medallions bring the instruments with which Christ will be tortured. From this allusion to Christ's future sufferings by means of iconographic details, the icon may be considered to be of the type known as the Virgin of the Passion. The epithet EPISKEPSIS ("Over-seer") does not refer to the iconographic type of the icon but to the human emotions often attributed to her in the 14th century, under the influence of retorical writings and liturgical poetry.

26 The Virgin with Christ, detail

Tempera on wood. 164.5 × 56 cm. c.1350. Dečani monastery, altar screen. Yugoslavia. Legends in Old Serbian.
Dečani is one of the few churches to have preserved five of the original altar-screen icons. Since the Dečani frescoes were painted for the Serbian king, later emperor, Dušan (1331–1355), in the mid-14th century, these preserved altar-screen icons are considered to date from the same time. The stylistic features of the icon, which depicts the Virgin and Child in tender embrace, also point to a period around 1350 as the possible date. The refined combination of purple, vermilion and gold with cool green tones, the attenuated proportions of the figures, and the confident draftsmanship of the body in movement show the master of the Dečani Virgin to have been a more gifted artist than many working in Serbia at that time.

27 The Virgin with Christ, gift of Archbishop Nicholas of Ohrid

Tempera on wood with revêtement. 91 × 53 cm. Mid-14th c. Ohrid, Icon Gallery, Yugoslavia. Legends in Greek, donor's inscription in Old Serbian.
In many respects this icon deviates from the Byzantine tradition: the red-haired Christ wears a greyish-white robe with an unusual neckline, while his cloak is orange-coloured – again very uncommon. The draftsmanship of the figures of mother and child suggests coastal rather than Byzantine models. The eyelashes of the Virgin are an extremely rare detail. The plaques with the evangelists in the Virgin's halo also differ from the late Byzantine tradition, for Mark is represented by a two-headed eagle. The standing figures of prophets, customary beside paintings of the Virgin, which ornament the silver frame, are executed in repoussé on thin silver sheet. The plaques with medallions in the lower right-hand corner were added later and do not belong to the original revêtement from the time when the icon was painted, on the orders of Archbishop Nicholas of Ohrid. His name and title were inscribed in red paste in the square fields on the right-hand border (NI)KOLA (e)P(i)S(ko)P. This well-known Ohrid archbishop may have commissioned the icon from some coastal master who was working in the interior. Since masters from Kotor on the southern Adriatic coast are known to have worked at Dečani, the Ohrid prelate may have made contact through the Serbian court with the artist whom he engaged to paint the icon.

28 The Presentation of the Virgin

Tempera on wood. 87 × 68.5 cm. Third quarter of the 14th c. Ohrid, Icon Gallery, Yugoslavia. Legends in Greek.
In the periods when artistic ties between the Balkans and Constantinople weakened, local workshops satisfied patrons' requirements. This was the case in Serbia after 1346, and also in Ohrid. This feast of the Virgin was painted, probably in the third quarter of the 14th century, on the reverse of a large ceremonial icon of the Virgin Peribleptos which had been brought to Ohrid earlier. The artist adhered to the established iconographic conventions, but was a far inferior draftsman and colourist to the painter of the obverse. The icon was carried in processions.

29 The Archangel Michael, called the Great Taxiarch

Tempera on wood. 110 × 81.5 cm. c. 1350–1360. Athens, Byzantine Museum. Legends in Greek.
This icon is thought to have formed part of a Deesis composition on an altar screen. The name Great Taxiarch draws attention to the archangel's senior rank in the celestial army. The cryptogram in the sphere held by the archangel is interpreted as "Christ the Righteous Judge". The highlighting with fine white hatching is typical of Byzantine painting in the 1360s, hence the dating of the icon to this period.

30 St Nicholas calming the Storm, detail from an icon of St Nicholas with scenes from his Life

Tempera on wood. Whole icon: 94.5 × 67 cm. Second half of the 14th c. Skopje, Museum of Macedonia, Yugoslavia. Legends in Greek.
This icon, found in St Sophia's in Ohrid, presents the saint in the customary fashion in the central field, surrounded by scenes from his Life. This episode illustrates one of the miracles ascribed to St Nicholas, celebrated as the protector of sailors. In its iconographic details, the scene follows the ancient Byzantine tradition transmitted in icon painting and legend for centuries.

31 Diptych of the Despotica Jelena

Carved wood with silver and gilded mount. 7.7 × 6.5 cm. 1368–1371. Treasury of Chilandar monastery on Mount Athos. Text in Old Serbian.
This small icon consists of two wings (diptych), each of which forms a separate entity. The central field of one contains a carving of the Virgin surrounded by prophets, and that of the other, the Holy Trinity with apostles. The busts of the prophets and apostles are set in finely carved vines. The outer sides of both wings in silver-gilt are engraved with a lament for the death of an only son. While living in Serres as the wife of Despot Uglješa Mrnjavčević, Jelena (Helen) showed a great love of literature and books. In her grief, she composed these verses for a diptych sent to Chilandar monastery on Athos, where her son, Uglješa, was interred. "These icons, though small, are a great gift, bearing the most sacred images of the Lord and the Most Pure Mother of God, given by a great lord and holy man to the infant Uglješa Despotović, whose undefiled young spirit has gone to its eternal home, while his body has been committed to the grave, because of the sins of Adam and Eve. Permit me, Lord Christ and You, Most Pure Mother of God, to concern myself in my misery with the departure of my soul, who has witnessed the deaths of my parents and young child, for whom my heart constantly grieves, as it is in a mother's nature to do." It is probable that Metropolitan Theodosius of Serres presented her infant son with these small icons, which Despotica Jelena later had remounted and set with jewels and pearls before sending them to Chilandar in 1371. Jelena also lost her husband in the battle on the Maritza against the Turks (1371), her home in Serres and the despotate. She became a nun, taking the name Euphemia (Jefimija) and living in Serbia in Ljubostinja convent and at the court of the Lazarevićs with Princess Milica (the nun Eugenia – Jevgenija), widow of Prince Lazar, killed in the battle of Kosovo (1389). Some later poems of the nun Jefimija, the first known Serbian poetess, have also been preserved.

32 The Virgin Kataphyge (Refuge) and St John the Theologian

Tempera on wood. 89 × 60 cm. c. 1371. Sofia, National Gallery. Legends and donor's inscription in Greek.
This bilateral processional icon has standing figures of the Virgin and St John the Theologian on the obverse, and on the reverse, the Vision of the Prophets Ezekiel and Habakkuk, modelled on a 5th-century mosaic composition preserved in the apse of the Salonican church of Hosios David. Between the Virgin and St John the donor's inscription is written in vermilion on the gold background. The actual name of the donor, a high-born woman, is missing. The section following the damaged part reads: "... to Christ God, the faithful lady (Vasilissa)". The icon was found at Poganovo monastery

near Pirot (Serbia) and taken to Sofia. Since the monastery is dedicated to St John the Theologian, this icon in which the apostle is shown with the Virgin is believed to have been specially painted for it. It was not, in fact, customary to depict these two figures together on a separate icon, though they can be found together on either side of the cross in the Crucifixion scene. The unusual subject and the Virgin's pose, her inclined head resting on her hand, as though caught in a moment of grief, can be ascribed to the influence of the donor, the distinguished lady mentioned in the inscription. The Virgin's epithet KATAPHYGE (Refuge) is not common on her icons, and suggests the influence of a patron inspired by liturgical poetry. Mentioned in the Greek inscription as "Vasilissa", she must have been the wife of a despot, and in any case was an educated noblewoman and connoisseur of the painting of her time. The icon's outstanding quality has long been noted, and led to it being ranked among the finest works of late Palaeologan art.

33 The Virgin Kataphyge (Refuge), detail of 32

The Virgin of Refuge is shown in the pose customary in pictures of the Crucifixion, where she is depicted grieving beneath the cross. The unusual epithet given to her here, however, has no connection with the iconography of the Crucifixion, and can only be explained as the choice of the donor, who must have been the wife of a despot since she is referred to as "Vasilissa". A painting of outstanding quality, this icon is considered one of the finest works of late Palaeologan art.

34 The Life of St Mary of Egypt

Tempera on wood. 25 × 29.5 cm. Late 14th c. Chilandar monastery on Mount Athos. Legends in Greek.
The Life of Mary of Egypt, written as early as the seventh century, is illustrated here in four rows without divisions between the episodes. Mary was an Alexandrian prostitute until her twenty-ninth year when, out of curiosity, she joined a ship of pilgrims bound for Jerusalem, having previously convinced the crew of the value of her services on the voyage. In the holy city, however, an angel forbade her to attend a church service. Mary, dumbfounded, turned to an icon of the Virgin and prayed for forgiveness, vowing to repent of her sins. She then withdrew into the deserts of Jordan and spent forty-seven years living as a hermit. Finally, as an infirm but serene old woman, she was found in the desert by an eminent Egyptian monk, Father Zosimas, who gave her Communion, himself astonished by her perseverance along the path of virtue. When he returned to the place a year later to give her Communion once more, he found her dead.
This Christian novella was often copied in manuscripts in the Middle Ages, but the subject was rarely depicted in icons. The painter may have used an illuminated manuscript of the Life of Mary of Egypt as his model for the icon. On the basis of stylistic features, it is considered to be the work of a Greek master from the late 14th century.

35 The Life of Mary of Egypt, detail of 34

Mary, an Alexandrian courtesan, asks the sailors to take her on the ship which is to transport pilgrims from Alexandria to the Holy Land, indicating the services she will render in return for her passage.

36 St Naum

Tempera on wood. 91.5 × 70.5 cm. Second half of the 14th c. Ohrid, Icon Gallery, Yugoslavia. Legend in Greek.
This bilateral processional icon has St Naum on the obverse, and on the reverse a much later painting (probably 18th c.) of the Archangel Michael. SS Clement and Naum, educators and Slav writers, were greatly venerated in Ohrid and the surroundings, and many medieval frescoes and icons celebrated their cult. This icon, which forms part of that tradition, was found in an Ohrid church dedicated to the Virgin (Bogorodica Bolnička), and was, it may be assumed, painted for one of the Ohrid churches. Its dating is based on stylistic elements.

37 St Clement

Tempera on wood. 86 × 65.5 cm. c. 1350. Ohrid, Icon Gallery, Yugoslavia. Legends in Greek.
The cult of the early Slav saint, Clement, was fostered in the churches of Ohrid and those under the jurisdiction of the Ohrid archbishopric. This Ohrid icon of St Clement, one of many preserved, was painted as a processional icon by an experienced artist who imbued it with the tendency towards idealization, spirituality, and the stylization of forms which were prevalent in Byzantine icon painting in the middle of the 14th century.

38 Jesus Christ, called Sotir and Zoodotis (Saviour and Giver of Life)

Tempera on wood. 131 × 88.5 cm. 1393/1394. Skopje, Museum of Macedonia, Yugoslavia. Legends and inscription in Greek.
The icon comes from the altar screen of the main church of Zrze monastery in Macedonia. Its precise date is recorded in the Greek inscription on the upper edge: "This icon of the Lord Christ was painted in the year 1393/1394." Only traces have survived of the inscription on the lower edge. The painter was Metropolitan Jovan (John), a noted prelate and artist, whose forebears had previously held the monastery and its estate in the village of Zrze, which in the early 15th century belonged to the countryman, Djurdjic. Metropolitan Jovan also painted frescoes in the church of St Andrew at Treska near Skopje, where he signed his work, together with his assistant, the monk Gregory, in 1389. An artist of exceptional education and talent, Metropolitan Jovan has left works that show an attempt, in those troubled times of Turkish invasion, to follow contemporary trends in Constantinopolitan painting, which in this period once more emphasized monumentality of figures with extremely plastic forms, modelled by finely hatched highlights, with gradual transition from dark shadow to pale ochre on the faces, necks and arms. Jovan's work marks him as a notable exponent of the late Palaeologan style.

39 St Demetrius

Tempera on wood. 34.5 × 26.5 cm. 15th c. Belgrade, Museum of Applied Arts. Legend in Greek.
The warrior saint is depicted with his weapons and accoutrement, to which the artist paid great attention. This elegant knight, fully equipped, is a frequent subject of fresco painters working in Serbian monasteries in the early 15th century. The harmonious proportions, colour scheme and manner of modelling the figure justify the proposed dating of this icon.

40 SS Sava and Simeon

Tempera on wood. 32.5 × 26 cm. 15th–16th c. Belgrade, National Museum. Legends and text on the scroll in Old Serbian.
The first two Serbian saints, St Simeon (Grand Prince Stefan Nemanja before becoming the monk Simeon) and his son St Sava (first archbishop of the autocephalous Serbian Church), were painted together in frescoes in Serbian churches from the early 14th century. The depiction of the founder of the Serbian state and the Nemanjić royal dynasty together with the founder of the Serbian archbishopric (1219) reflects the desire of learned Serbian archbishops to strengthen their independence and safeguard it from the Byzantine Church by glorifying the cult of these Serbian saints. The cult of St Simeon, established in Serbia as early as the beginning of the 13th century, and that of St Sava, established immediately after his death (1235), were particularly fostered at Chilandar, the monastery they had founded on Mount Athos. The icon is dated on the basis of stylistic features to the 15th or 16th century.

41 The Virgin Pelagonitissa, by the hieromonk Makarije

Tempera on wood. 134 × 93.5 cm. 1421/1422. Skopje, Museum of Macedonia, Yugoslavia. Legends in Greek, and inscription referring to the painter and donor in Old Serbian.
The icon comes from the iconostasis of Zrze monastery in Macedonia. The well-preserved inscription on the upper edge reads: "By the will of our Lord and God and Saviour, and by the grace of the immaculate Virgin, this holy image was painted in this year of 1421/1422. In honour of our Lord by the hieromonk Master Makarije, painter." Another inscription along the lower edge mentions the donor of the icon and his family: "The prayer of God's servant Konstantin, son of Djurdjić and grandson of Šagman, and his wife Mistress Teodora, and his sons Jakov and Kalojan and Dmitar, and daughters Ana and Jela. Remember, O Lord, also his parents and his brother Bogoje who died in captivity and his daughter Mistress Zoja." From other sources, Makarije (Makarios) is known to have been the brother of the painter Metropolitan Jovan, and a descendant of the family which founded the monastery in the mid-14th century. After the Turkish conquest of Macedonia, he moved to the Serbian state centred on the Morava river valley and worked at Ljubostinja convent, but later returned to his homeland. This icon of the Virgin with Christ bearing the epithet Pelagonitissa, showing the playful infant in his mother's arms, was painted by Makarije for the renovated iconostasis commissioned for Zrze monastery by the Djurdjić family. Since many icons of the same type and with the same epithet (Pelagonian) have been preserved – for example, the one in the 13th-century Serbian Prizren Gospels, the one in fresco technique on the altar screen of St George's church at Staro Nagoričino (1318), those painted on wood and preserved at Dečani (14th c.), and in Prizren (14th c.), and that in the 15th-century church of St Nicholas in Prilep, now in Skopje (44) – there is believed to have been a very ancient and venerated icon of the Virgin and Child of this type, well known to all, which acquired its epithet from its place of origin. All later versions painted to celebrate this cult, already widespread in the region of Pelagonia, retained the iconographic features of the original. As regards stylistic qualities, these varied with the artistic concepts prevalent in a particular period and the skill of the artist. The Virgin Pelagonitissa by Makarije is notable for the very dark skin tones and stylized facial features, reflecting the 15th-century tendency to idealization and dematerialization of holy figures. Scant attention is paid to volume, the emphasis being placed on contours. Despite his inadequate grasp of anatomy and excessive attention to drapery, Makarije was clearly a painter familiar with works of greater artistic value, which he endeavoured to emulate.

42 The Virgin with Christ, known as Petrovskaya

Tempera on wood. 31 × 25.5 cm. 15th c. Zagorsk, Museum (Holy Trinity-Sergiev monastery), Soviet Union. Legends in Greek.
This type of small icon intended for individual prayer was privately owned and brought to the monastery together with the body of the deceased at the time of burial. This particular icon is known to have belonged to the Princess Paraskovya (Iraida before she became a nun), the second wife of Prince Danil Borisovich Priimkov-Rostovski, who was buried in the Sergiev monastery in 1582. From its style, it is assumed to have come from one of the Moscow workshops where dark skin-tones and emphasis on outline predominated in the 15th century. Russian icon painters long remained faithful to a style characterized by pronounced linearism and stylization of forms.

43 Christ Immanuel

Tempera on wood with revêtement. 26 × 21 cm. 15th c. Zagorsk, Museum (Holy Trinity-Sergiev monastery), Soviet Union. Legend in Old Russian.
This small icon was brought to Holy Trinity-Sergiev monastery at the time of the burial of its owner, Fyodor Vasilyevich Korobov (1556), who was present at the marriage of Ivan the Terrible and Anastasia Romanovna in 1547. Its style indicates that it came from

a 15th-century Moscow workshop. The stylized face, in which line is the main means of expression and volume is neglected, is typical of Russian icons of this period. The painter stresses only the eyes, which hold the attention of the viewer, leading his thoughts into the immaterial, abstract spheres of religious doctrine.

44 The Virgin with Christ, of the type known as Pelagonitissa

Tempera on wood. 79 × 47 cm. 15th–16th c. Skopje, Museum of Macedonia, Yugoslavia. A processional icon found in the church of St Nicholas in Prilep. In this town and throughout the region of Pelagonia, the old icon of the Virgin Pelagonitissa provided a major source of inspiration for many icon painters over several centuries. It illustrates how one iconographic type could retain its popularity for a lengthy period in a particular region, since the cult of the oldest icon of this type was long celebrated in a local church (cf. 41). This version of the Virgin with Christ is also known as the "Playful Infant". The anonymous painter of this icon, which was undoubtedly made for a church in Pelagonia, perhaps the Prilep church where it was found, was not a skilful draftsman. He was incapable of depicting convincingly the movements of the infant, or even the anatomical contours of the static figure of the mother beneath her dark robe. The folds of the drapery, painted with innumerable tiny lines, do not suggest the form of the body, but are treated rather as ornamentation covering an extensive area of the picture. Nevertheless, by enlarging the figures of the Virgin and Child, which fill most of the painted surface of the icon, and contrasting them with the extremely small figures of angels, their hands covered respectfully, that face the Virgin in the upper corners, the master managed to achieve a certain monumentality. The exaggerated plasticity of the uncovered parts of the bodies and the almost flat treatment of the clothed parts are the mark of an unskilled and uneducated provincial painter, whose work is redeemed by a certain naive freshness. Compared with the icon of the Virgin Pelagonitissa from Prizren (14th c.), with the icon painted by the hieromonk Makarije in 1421/1422 (41), or with others of that type, this is a far less skilful and sophisticated work, and demonstrates how the early 14th-century classicist style of icon painting degenerated into the folk art of isolated provincial workshops.

45 Scene from an icon of St George: The Raising of Glicarius' Oxen

Tempera on wood. Whole icon: 134 × 74.5 cm. 15th–16th c. Struga, Church of St George, Yugoslavia. Legends in Greek.
This scene is one episode in the Life of St George, illustrated, according to the Byzantine iconographic tradition, in a series of scenes around the central standing figure of the saint. The episode depicted here is one of the miracles attributed to St George, who was celebrated as the protector of farmers.

46 The Crucifixion, by the painter Dionisi

Tempera on wood. 85 × 52 cm. c. 1500. Moscow, Tretyakov Gallery. Legends in Old Russian.
This icon from the main church of Holy Trinity Pavlov-Obnorski monastery, considered to be one of the finest examples of Russian icon painting, is by an artist whose works were greatly admired by his contemporaries and later generations. He was trained in Moscow workshops in the mid-15th century, when followers of the celebrated Russian icon painter, Andrei Rublev, were still working there. The Crucifixion, one of the row of the Twelve Feasts on the altar screen of Holy Trinity monastery, displays all Dionisi's mastery, with the characteristic linear rhythm of the dematerialized elongated figures, placed on a narrow zone of barely indicated landscape before the walls of Jerusalem. The refined shading and light brush-strokes are the marks of an outstanding artist. The perfectly balanced composition with its pale colours and the gentle radiance of the gold background evoke a feeling of profound serenity.

47 Christ, called Sotir (the Saviour)

Tempera on wood. 73 × 41 cm. Early 16th c. Skopje, Museum of Macedonia, Yugoslavia. Legend in Greek.
This icon from the church of St John Kaneo at Ohrid is the work of an artist much influenced by 14th-century painting. He used gold and was successful in his modelling of the face, with its gradual transitions from dark shadows to pale ochre and rosy tints, but his disregard of anatomy indicates a 16th-century master trained in a provincial workshop in the Balkans.

48 The Descent from the Cross

Tempera on wood. Part of the border of an icon of the Virgin Enthroned measuring 86.5 × 67.5 cm. Early 16th c. Athens, Benaki Museum.
This extremely restrained, austere picture is constructed on the principle of the harmony of cool green and warm red tones, which in this symmetrical composition heightens the static effect. By these means the anonymous artist created an impression of monumentality despite the small size of the scene. Faithfully following the old Byzantine tradition in both iconography and style, this exceptionally talented artist remained far removed from developments in Renaissance Europe.

49 The Dormition of the Virgin, by the painter Dmitar

Tempera on wood. 73 × 36.5 cm. Fourth decade of the 16th c. Skopje, Museum of Macedonia, Yugoslavia. Legends and texts on the scrolls in Greek.
This icon from Slepče monastery near Bitola (Macedonia) is signed in the upper left-hand corner, above the frame of the composition. Master Dmitar repeated a very ancient version of the scene of the Virgin's death with the figures of the Byzantine poets, John of Damascus and Cosmas of Maiuma, in separate fields. Both celebrated the cult of the

Virgin in many of their verses, and for this reason were depicted in this manner beside the scene of the Virgin's death in earlier painting, for example at Bachkovo (12th c.) in Bulgaria and in other churches. In addition to the figures traditionally shown as present at this event, such as apostles, bishops and Christ receiving the Virgin's soul, Dmitar introduced these two religious poets, following some less common iconographic variants. Clumsy draftsmanship and failure to impart radiance to his figures by the use of more glowing tones mark Dmitar, nevertheless, as a provincial master who sought his model and guidance from tradition.

50 The Virgin Mary, known as Vladimirskaya

Tempera on wood with revêtement. 32.5 × 25.5 cm. Early 16th c. Zagorsk, Museum (Holy Trinity-Sergiev monastery), Soviet Union. Legends in Greek.
This icon was privately owned until 1514, when it came into the possession of Holy Trinity monastery. It was named Vladimirskaya since it repeated the iconographic type of the famous Russian icon known as the Virgin of Vladimir, which was specially venerated as early as the late 11th or early 12th century. Many later icons were painted for the purpose of celebrating this ancient cult. As a rule, such small icons for private prayer were richly sheathed with silver-gilt with embossed or filigree ornamentation and precious stones. Pearls enhance the brilliance of this setting. The anonymous artist was obviously trained in the tradition of Byzantine icon painting.

51 The Crowning of St George

Tempera on wood. 80 × 52.5 cm. 16th c. Sofia, National Art Gallery, Bulgaria. Legend in Greek.
The crowning of the holy warrior and martyr was a popular subject in late Byzantine painting. An angel, as a celestial messenger, places a wreath, with Christ's blessing, on the head of the martyr, whose feat has earned him the reward of eternal life. The iconographic formula of these pictures originated in antiquity, the depiction of the lives of saints, illustrated in frescoes or icons, always appears when suffering for the faith is a dominant theme. The icon found in Plovdiv belongs to this tradition, recalling the holy warrior's acceptance of martyrdom by refusing to serve in an army led by a Roman emperor. From the Comnenian period on, such scenes of the crowning of the holy warriors, George and Demetrius, are very common in Byzantine and post-Byzantine art.

52 The Virgin with Christ, called Kecharitomeni (Full of Grace) with scenes from her Life

Tempera on wood. 106 × 83 cm. 16th c. Sofia, Church Museum. Legends in Greek.
The icon represents the Virgin with Christ flanked by eight scenes from her Life, and surmounted by the Deesis composition. The epithet "Full of Grace" was given to the Virgin as one of the traditional epithets, taken in earlier centuries from Byzantine liturgical poetry, and repeated in frescoes and icons. This is a processional icon: the groove for the pole can be seen on the lower edge and it has a painting of the Crucifixion on the reverse. The artist probably took some fine old icon as his model, but turned the folds of the Virgin's robe into sharp ornamental lines, while the shading of the flesh contrasts crudely with the lighter surfaces.

53 The Birth of the Virgin, detail of 52

The scene of the Virgin's birth is part of the usual cycle of her Life. The bringing of gifts to her mother, Anne, the bathing of the infant and the cradle are customary details of the scene, which was presented in this manner for centuries in Byzantine art.

54 Royal doors, by the painter Georgije Mitrofanović

Tempera on wood with wood-carving. 1620. Chilandar monastery on Mount Athos. Legends in Old Serbian.
The doors are part of the iconostasis of the chapel of St Tryphon, which stands outside the monastery walls, close to the entrance. With their combined resources, the hierodeacons Isaiah and Michael and the Chilandar monk Georgije (George) Mitrofanović donated a new, carved iconostasis for this chapel, on which Georgije painted the icons and royal doors. In this period his painting attained the beauty to which he had long aspired. His draftsmanship and the proportions of the figures have been perfected, the colours are richer, and the modelling of the faces is achieved by very delicate shading. These doors rank among the finest of Georgije's later works. The artist's very large opus includes many icons and frescoes preserved in the churches of Old Herzegovina, Dalmatia and Serbia, where he worked between 1615/1616 and 1620.

55 Head of the Virgin Mary, detail of 54

From the Comnenian period of Byzantine art, if not earlier, the Annunciation was traditionally painted on the royal doors, which gave the clergy access to the altar region from the nave. Georgije Mitrofanović, a Chilandar monk and painter, followed this tradition when painting the two wings of the royal doors of the iconostasis of the chapel of St Tryphon at Chilandar. The busts of the prophets David and Solomon above the Virgin and the Archangel Gabriel are connected with the scene by the same long-established custom. With its respect for tradition in the choice of subjects and in iconographic solutions, the painting of Georgije Mitrofanović was very close to that of contemporary Greek masters, following the work of the so-called Italo-Cretan Greek painters, who were then considered the most advanced in the eastern Christian world.

56 Carved and painted cross

Tempera on wood. 197 × 187 cm. 16th c. Church of St John the Baptist in the village of Slepče, Yugoslavia. Legends in Old Serbian.

In many Orthodox churches crosses have been preserved on the top of altar screens, where they were traditionally placed from the very earliest period of Byzantine art. In the 16th century these crosses were usually of painted wood, embellished with carving and gilded. They depict the crucified Christ, and very often, as in this cross at Slepče (Macedonia), include the symbols of the evangelists on the arms of the cross. Similar crosses, an essential element of the very high and elaborate altar screens, were produced in this period in many Balkan and Athonite workshops. The Virgin and St John the Theologian, figures always present in scenes of the Crucifixion, were frequently painted on separate panels placed below the cross. The Slepče cross, a work of this type, is notable for its fine carving and well-preserved painted surfaces in warm tones.

57 St John the Baptist, gift of Metropolitan Ilarion

Tempera on wood. 63.3 × 42.5 cm. 1644. Belgrade, Museum of the Serbian Orthodox Church. Legends and inscriptions in Old Serbian.
This icon comes from Krušedol monastery in the Srem region of Yugoslavia. It depicts St John the Baptist (Forerunner) with wings and holding his own head on a platter in his left hand, with which he also supports a long cross. These attributes and the angelic expression of the saint derive from iconographic models well known since the end of the 13th century, when they had became popular under the influence of Byzantine liturgical poetry. Two texts are preserved in the lower part of the icon: one on a scroll (lines from the sticheron [hymn] sung at vespers on the eve of the feast of the Beheading of John), and the other around it, on the lower edge of the icon. This latter records the date of its painting and the name of the donor: "Completed on the 29th day of November, 1644. Donated by the most reverend Metropolitan of Belgrade and Srem, Kyr Ilarion. May God have mercy on him."

58 St Marina

Tempera on wood with carving. 17th c. Sofia, Church Museum. Legend in Bulgarian.
Wood-carving flourished in Balkan workshops during the late Middle Ages. The royal doors and crosses of iconostases, in particular, were richly carved with vegetable and geometrical ornamentation, gilded and painted. The figure of St Marina, earlier painted at the entrance of a church as the protectress against evil and demonic powers, in time was also depicted on certain royal doors, as the guardian of the entrace to the altar region, or on icons decorated with carved frames, as on this one found in Plovdiv.

59 St Anne and the Virgin, by Emmanuel Tzanes

Tempera on wood. 106 × 76 cm. 1637. Athens, Benaki Museum. Legends in Greek.
The date and the artist's signature are inscribed on this icon, which testifies to the exceptionally long survival of ancient forms in the Mediterranean Greek workshops, particularly on the island of Crete. The so-called Italo-Cretan masters continued to supply icons to Orthodox patrons in the Mediterranean region after the fall of Constantinople to the Turks down to the late 17th and 18th centuries. Whereas in the 18th century artists were already introducing Baroque features in their work and changing the old iconography, such attempts were much rarer in the 17th century. The flower held by the young Virgin as a symbol of Christ is not a customary detail in medieval Byzantine icons. However, the method of painting and modelling flesh, the pose of the mother and child, and harmony of colour mark Emmanuel Tzanes as a faithful follower of the earlier great masters of Byzantine art.

60 The Entry of Christ into Jerusalem, by the painter Longin

Tempera on wood. 22.5 × 35.5 cm. 1578/1579. Lomnica monastery, Yugoslavia. Legends in Old Serbian.
Thanks to the inscriptions left by the artist, Longin, on the icons he painted for the iconostasis of the main church of Lomnica monastery (Bosnia), we know that this work was completed in 1578/1579. The icons were cleaned some years ago and returned to the iconostasis at Lomnica. In the lower row are the two main icons: of the Virgin with Christ, angels and prophets, and of Christ, while the upper range comprises smaller icons of the Twelve Feasts, one of which is illustrated here. After finishing the icons for the iconostasis, Longin began work on the frescoes in the same church, but did not complete them.
Longin, a monk at Peć monastery, was a poet as well as a much sought after artist. He painted many icons in Peć, Dečani, Piva, Velika Hoča and other churches in the territory of the restored patriarchate of Peć, which after 1557 exerted a powerful influence on the revival of cultural life among the Serbs. Thanks to the religious toleration of the Ottoman

Empire in the second half of the 16th century, icon painting flourished in Serbian lands. Master Longin developed his talent in the Serbian monastic environment of that time. When learning to paint, he relied mainly on examples of early 14th-century Serbian painting. His composition of scenes, enclosed by high hills or painted architecture, his traditional arrangement of dark-robed figures in the foreground, set against the bright slopes of hills or against an ochre or gold background, his fine modelling of flesh with light shading, and his fresh colours, all show Longin to have been a gifted master of Serbian icon painting of the late 16th century.

61 St George Slaying the Dragon, gift of the hieromonk Vasilije

Tempera on wood. 88 × 63 cm. 1667. Sofia, Art Gallery. Inscription in Bulgarian.
The icon, brought from Kremikovtsi monastery, has an inscription mentioning all those who were involved in the procuring of the icon. In this late period, numerous donors might join together to commission an icon. The painter, though of modest skill and knowledge, displays a feeling for fresh, clear colours in this traditional version of St George slaying the dragon and freeing the princess, which was painted for the hieromonk Vasilije and his relatives or friends.

62 The Archangel Michael

Tempera on wood with carved frame. 61 × 43 cm. with the frame. 1742. Church of St Michael at Sentandre, Hungary. Legends in Serbian.
The unknown artist painted this main icon for the iconostasis of what was called the Požarevac church dedicated to St Michael in Sentandre. Since all the icons of this large iconostasis are very similar in style, the year 1742 inscribed on the icon of the Nativity is considered to be the date when the whole iconostasis was raised, and all the icons for it painted. The icons of this church, ascribed to two anonymous masters, display certain Baroque features. These new Baroque influences are presumed to have reached the Serbian eparchy of Buda and Sentandre via Walachia, by way of the Serbs who maintained contacts with the Romanians and followed the development of religious art in the brancovan epoch.

63 Part of the iconostasis of the church of St Michael in Sentandre, Hungary

In the 18th century the Eastern Orthodox churches acquired very high wooden iconostases decorated with carving and painted icons. On this one in the Serbian "Požarevac" church dedicated to St Michael in Sentandre (Hungary), the anonymous artists painted six main icons in the lower row, the Deesis with the twelve apostles above them, and in the third row, sixteen icons of prophets, surmounted by a cross with the Crucifixion and icons of the Virgin and St John the Theologian. The royal doors consist of eighteen medallions containing figures of the prophets, forming the composition of the Tree of Jesse. In Byzantine iconography, this traditional composition explained the origin of the Virgin and Christ, and therefore it appeared on the royal doors below the subjects of the Annunciation and the Baptism of Christ, which are depicted at the top of the two wings. The Baroque forms of the vines linking the medallions and certain Baroque elements of the painting herald a new era in Serbian art and the tentative acceptance by the Serbian population in Austro-Hungarian towns of a style which was not Byzantine, and which had long been flourishing in western Europe.

64 Part of a templon with holy figures: Elijah with Elisha and St Theodore

Tempera on wood with wood-carving. 17th c. Sofia, Church Museum. Legends in Greek.
In the late Middle Ages in the Balkans, iconostases were frequently decorated with carving, gilding and relief ornamentation. This part of a templon, the painted wooden panel attached to the architrave of the iconostasis, depicts mounted holy warriors. The clumsily drawn horses, the saints too large for their steeds, the architecture and landscape, and the schematic figures, all very similar, are the marks of a craftsman with scant artistic training, but his fresh, clear colours and feeling for the decorative satisfied the taste of his time and his patrons.
In writings from the second half of the 6th century there is a rapid increase in the number of legends about miracle-working icons of Christ and the Virgin Mary, and of reports of veneration of icons. Pagan beliefs and superstitions and many old customs were grafted onto the new cults. From the works of St Augustine (5th c.), who was opposed to the depiction of the divinity, we learn that a certain Marcellina worshipped Christ, St Paul, Homer and Pythagoras, burning incense before their images. In the sixth and seventh centuries, reports by writers and pilgrims on the burning of incense are ever more numerous; clearly the ancient customs and forms of worship were repeated before the icons of Christ, the Virgin Mary and the saints.

4

СТЫ
IΩА
НЪ

ПРО
ДРО
МЪ

+ПОКАНТ
ЕСЕПРИБЛ
НЖНБОСЕ
РСТВОҐЕСК
ОЕҐОЖЕБОС
ѢКНРАПР
НКОРѢНЕ
ДРѢВАЛЕ
ЖНТЪНЕ
ТВОРЕШЕ
ПЛОДАГ
СЕВАЕТ

6

9

13

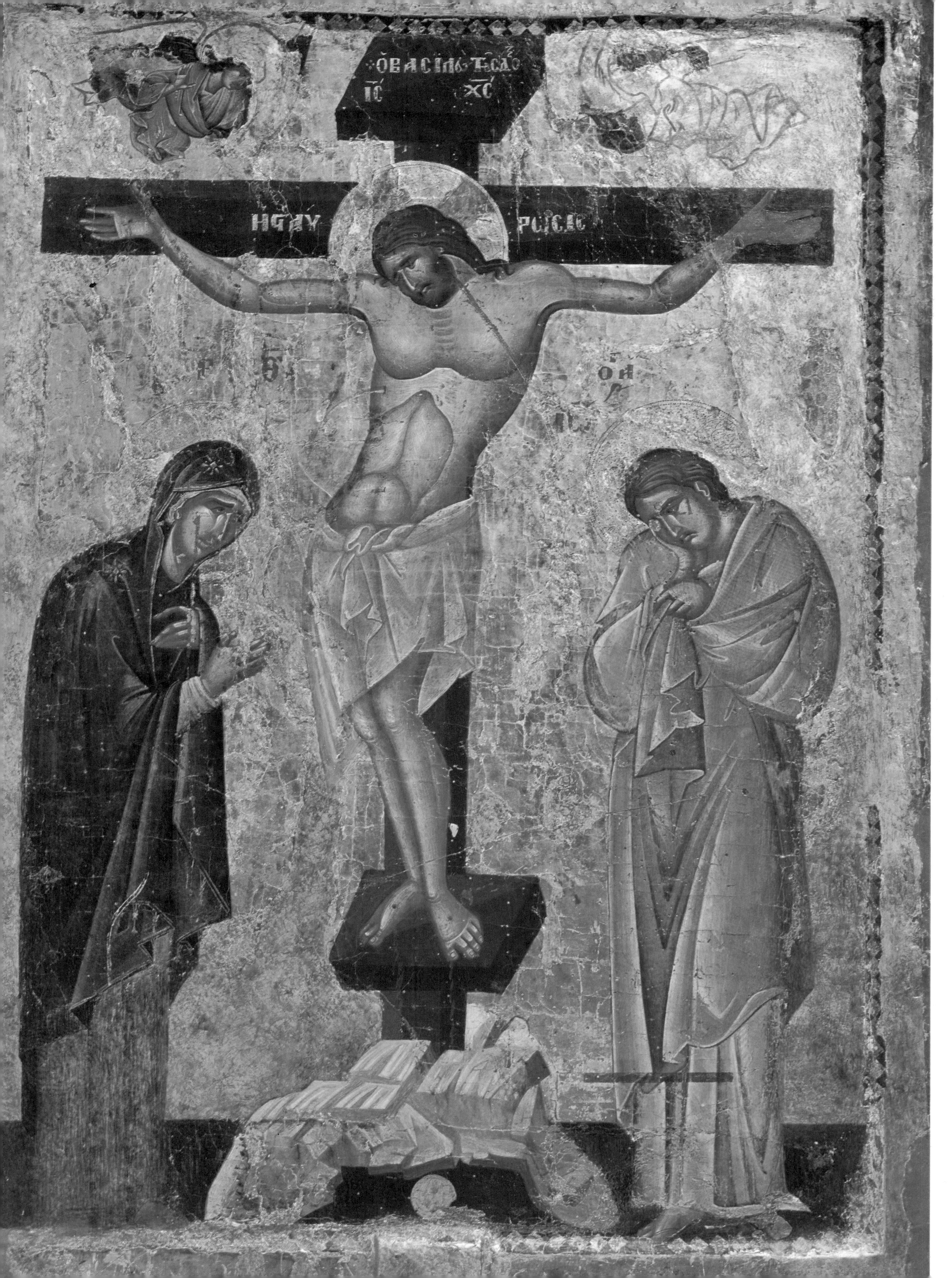
IC XC

Ὁ ἉΓΙΟΣ ΜΑΤΘΑΙΟΣ

16

17

31

34

Ο Α ΔΜΗ ... ΤΙ ΟС

ΜΡ ΘΥ

ΙC ΧC

Η ΠΕΛΑΓΟΝΙΤΙCΑ

43

44

ĪC ō XC

Ὁ ⲤⲰ ⲦⲎⲢ·

ΔΕΥΤΕΟⲨ
ⲈⲨΛⲞⲄⲈ
ⲘΕΝΟΙ·Τ
ΠⲢⲤΜΟⲨ
ΚΛΗⲢΟ

ΝΟΜΕⲦ
ⲤΑΤΕΤ
ΗΤΗΙ
ⲤΜΕΝΟΙ
ΗΜΙΝΒ

48

52

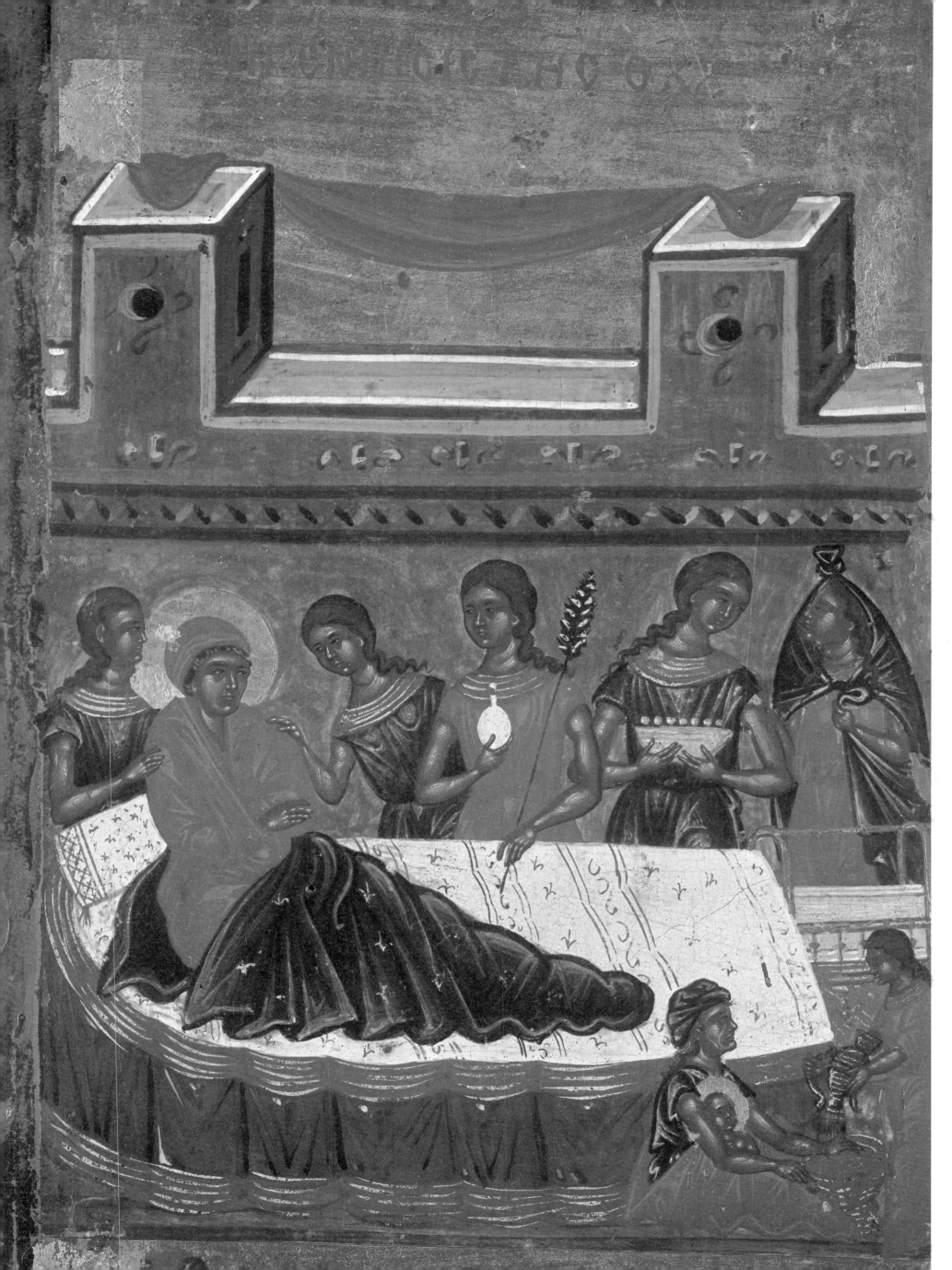